On July 28, 1976, Terry Fox is eighteen years old. He has an "Athlete of the Year" award from his school in Port Coquitlam, British Columbia. His family are very happy. Five years later, Terry is dead.

Today, his statue stands in Ottawa. Betty Fox looks at it and remembers. Her son is a Canadian hero. This is his story.

1

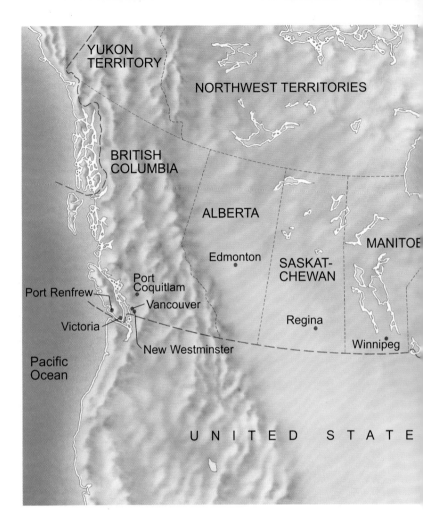

At eighteen, Terry Fox is a good student and a strong athlete. The happy times stop in March, 1977. One day, Terry is running home. He stops suddenly. His mother looks out the window. "It's my right leg," Terry says. The family takes him to the hospital. Terry has cancer and there is only one answer. On March 9, the doctors operate. Three weeks later, Terry has an artificial leg.

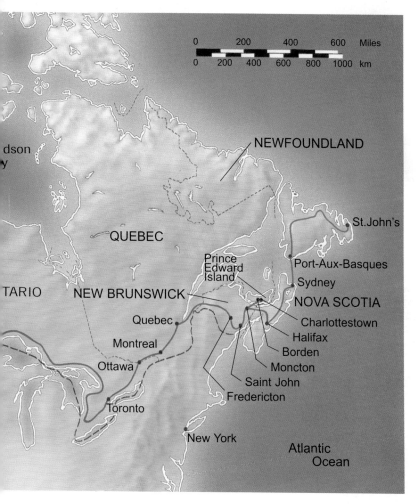

Terry goes home in April, but he often thinks of the children with cancer in the hospital. "Only money can stop the pain," he thinks. He remembers a story about a man with one leg in the New York Marathon. "I can do that," Terry says. "I can run across Canada for money." "You can't run from the Atlantic to the Pacific Ocean on one good leg," his mother says. But Terry doesn't listen.

3

Terry calls his run, the "Marathon of Hope." It is a long
road. From St. John's to Port Renfrew is 5,300 miles
(8,530 km). Terry can't start in 1977. But early in 1979,
he is running every day. One year later, he is strong again.
Terry's marathon starts at St. John's, Newfoundland, on
April 12, 1980. His friend, Doug Alward, is his driver.
Terry runs in the day. At night, he sleeps in the car.

The marathon starts well. "Newfoundland has two
things," Terry says, "the ocean and people." He likes
running near water, and the people are very friendly. He
and Doug don't always sleep in the car. They often stay
in houses or hotels. People don't take money from them.
Terry runs 550 miles (885 km) in twenty-three days. In
Port-Aux-Basques, the people of the town give $8,000.

Terry arrives in Sydney, Nova Scotia, on May 7. The newspapers don't know about him and there are no people in the streets. He doesn't stop.

On May 8, he is on the road to Halifax. He runs early in the morning. "I like that quiet time of day," he says. But he gets angry with Doug and Doug doesn't talk to him. Terry's family are unhappy about this.

Betty and Rolly Fox go to Halifax. They talk to Doug and
Terry. After this, the two young men are friends again.
Terry finishes his first 1,000 miles (1,609 km). Then he
goes to Prince Edward Island. It is a beautiful place and
people are very friendly. On the road from Borden, they
give $600. On May 26, a happy Terry talks to 900
students at a school in Charlottetown.

On May 28, Terry is near Moncton, New Brunswick. He can't sleep and he is often in pain from his artificial leg. "See a doctor," Doug says. Terry says no. He sends his leg to a man in Fredericton. A day later, he can run again. On May 31, he arrives in St. John. His brother, Darrell, is waiting for him. "Now I'm with the marathon, too," Darrell says. That night, Terry is happy again.

In Quebec, the three young men have a problem. They
don't understand French. For Terry, it is bad on the
road, too. Some drivers drive very near him.

On June 24, he arrives in Montreal. There, he meets
Isadore Sharp. They stay in his hotel, The Four Seasons.
He gives $2 for every mile of the marathon. He has an
important message for all Canadians: "Give money."

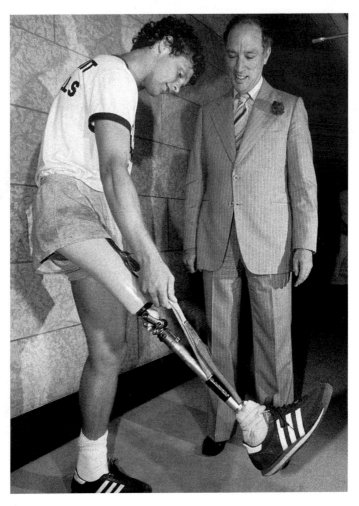

The people of Ontario listen to Isadore's message and give $1,000,000. Terry is now famous. He meets the Canadian prime minister, Pierre Trudeau, in Ottawa on June 30. After this, people call his name in every town. Terry doesn't like it. "OK, I'm famous," he says in Toronto. "But I'm not running for that. Think about the sick children. Think about the 'Marathon of Hope.'"

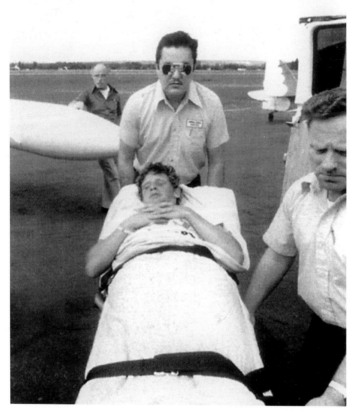

After Toronto, Terry doesn't run well. In the evenings,
he isn't strong and he often can't talk to people. "See a
doctor," Darrell says. Again, Terry says no.

On September 1, Terry is running near Thunder Bay.
There is a bad pain in his lungs. After a mile, he stops.
An airplane takes him back home. He goes to the
hospital in New Westminster.

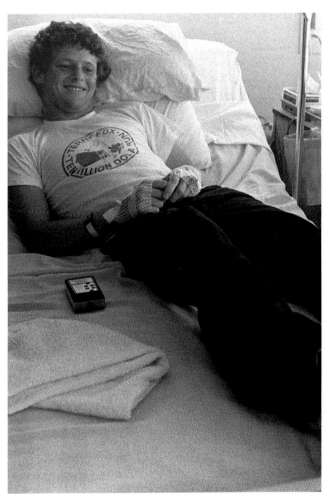

The "Marathon of Hope" stops 3,339 miles (5,372km) from St. John's, Newfoundland. Terry can't finish his long road, but there is now $1,400,000 for sick children. This is good—but Terry has cancer again. This time it is in his lungs. In a big TV show, on September 9, famous people say thank you to Canada's hero. Terry watches from his bed and smiles.

After the TV show, Canadians and Americans give
$10,000,000. Ten days later, Terry gets the "Order of
Canada," the country's number one award. Important
people say thank you to him. Betty and Rolly sit with
Terry and listen. They smile, but they aren't happy.
Their son is now very sick. The doctors can't stop
Terry's cancer.

Terry Fox dies on June 28, 1981. Letters come to the family from around the world. "We are very sorry about Terry," they say. Pierre Trudeau calls him "Canada's hero." Isadore Sharp remembers him, too.

"Money from Terry's marathon brings hope to all people with cancer," he says. "Now it is our fight. Can we run a marathon for cancer in Terry's name every year?"

The answer is yes. The first Terry Fox Run in Canada
starts in week three of September, 1981. It brings
$3,500,000 to the fight with cancer.

Today, there are Terry Fox Runs around the world. In
the same week in September every year, people run and
remember "Canada's hero." Terry is dead, but his
message is always with us: "Stop the pain."

ACTIVITIES

Before you read

1 Look at the pictures in the book and answer the questions.

   a Where is Terry Fox from?

   b Why is he famous?

2 Find the words in your dictionary.

   around   artificial   athlete   award   cancer   die   fight
   hero   hope   hospital   lungs   marathon   message   mile
   operate   pain   prime minister   show (n)   *statue   world*

   a Find the words for people.

   b Find the words for places.

After you read

3 Answer the questions about Terry Fox.

   a Where does Terry's "Marathon of Hope" start?

   b Where does the marathon finish?

   c Why does Terry run the marathon?

   d Why does he stop?

   e When is the first Terry Fox Run?

4 "Terry Fox is a hero for all sick people, not only people with cancer."
   Talk about this.

5 You work for a newspaper. Write a story about day one of Terry's
   marathon.

6 Write a letter to Terry's family about their son.

SECOND EDITION

MW01064752

LIFESTYLE ANALYSIS IN DIVORCE CASES

INVESTIGATING SPENDING AND
FINDING HIDDEN INCOME AND ASSETS

TRACY COENEN, CPA, CFF

AMERICAN**BAR**ASSOCIATION

Family Law Section

Cover design by Kelly Book/ABA Design

To the man who changed my mind about marriage. I love you forever.

Contents

Chapter 5
Financial Discovery

Chapter 6
Documents Used in the Lifestyle Analysis

About the Author

Tracy Coenen, CPA, CFF of Sequence Inc. Forensic Accounting has spent more than 20 years investigating fraud. Her educational background includes an Honors Bachelor of Arts in Criminology and Law Studies and a Master of Business Administration, both from Marquette University. Tracy is a Certified Public Accountant and holds the designations Certified in Financial Forensics and Master Analyst in Financial Forensics.

She has personally investigated hundreds of frauds in a wide variety of industries, including cases of embezzlement, financial statement fraud, investment fraud, divorce, and insurance fraud. She has also served as an expert witness in numerous cases involving damage calculations, commercial contract disputes, shareholder disputes, and criminal defense.

Tracy has been an adjunct instructor at Marquette University, adjunct professor at Concordia University, adjunct faculty member for the Association of Certified Fraud Examiners (ACFE), and faculty member for the National Association of Certified Valuators and Analysts (NACVA). She is the author of three books: *Expert Fraud Investigation: A Step-by-Step Guide*, *Essentials of Corporate Fraud*, and *Lifestyle Analysis in Divorce Cases: Investigating Spending and Finding Hidden Income and Assets*.

Chapter 1

Purpose of the Lifestyle Analysis

Numbers in Family Law Cases

Accounting is a topic that can frighten otherwise brave professionals. All the asset, liability, income, and expense talk can be overwhelming if the listener is not trained in the field of accounting. Even those who have taken a couple of accounting courses can get bogged down in the details and have a difficult time translating the numbers and determining what they really mean to a case.

The best forensic accountants are able to present financial issues in litigation so they can be understood readily. Attorneys, judges, and juries often lack an accounting or finance background, so being able to break down financial topics in a way that is easy to understand is essential for forensic accountants. The best expert witnesses are those who can relate to the judge and jury and who can make sense of even the most complex numbers.

Family law cases involving complex financial matters often require the assistance of a financial expert for the following issues:

- Preparing a financial disclosure, including creating a marital balance sheet
- Comparing balance sheets from period to period to evaluate changes in assets and liabilities and to determine the reasons for those changes
- Analyzing financial disclosures or affidavits prepared by the spouses to determine accuracy, completeness, and changes over time

1

- Calculating the historical income of the spouses
- Evaluating the prospects for future income of the spouses, including estimating future wages and business income
- Determining income (or the ability to pay) to calculate spousal support or child support
- Determining the standard of living (or the need for support) of the spouses and children
- Valuing business entities or other assets (such as real estate or pensions)
- Identifying assets and determining whether they are nonmarital (separate) or subject to division (marital or community)
- Tracing and finding funds or other assets
- Analyzing claims of dissipation, wasteful spending, or fraudulent conveyance
- Evaluating the income tax impact of various scenarios related to asset division and support payments
- Assessing the work of an opposing financial expert to determine its accuracy or to write a rebuttal report
- Providing other litigation assistance, such as assisting with drafting discovery demands and interrogatories or preparing for the depositions of individuals with financial information

In addition to these financial issues, an accounting expert could also play the following roles in family law cases:

- Assisting with settlement activities, evaluating the financial impact of a settlement offer, making certain calculations, and giving opinions on various settlement scenarios
- Mediating a divorce case with financial issues to help the parties reach a settlement
- Acting as a neutral expert in the divorce, providing an objective opinion on financial matters. The parties may agree together on the financial neutral, or the court may appoint the accountant.
- Participating in post-court activity and aiding in the evaluation of financial disputes, including things like allegations of fraud during the divorce process or motions for modification of support

Although a financial expert can be involved in family law cases in many different ways, this book focuses on determining income, determining the standard of living, identifying assets, and tracing and finding funds or other assets. The work may be done because of allegations of hidden income or assets, but many times it is done simply because of a need to determine income and expenses when the parties are unable to do so without the assistance of an expert.

Choosing a Financial Professional

There are a number of different types of financial professionals who might get involved in family law cases, including

- Certified Public Accountants (CPAs)
- Forensic accountants (who may or may not be CPAs)
- Accountants or bookkeepers
- Investment analysts or advisors
- Financial planners
- Business valuators
- Appraisers
- Actuaries

This book focuses on the work of forensic accountants because that is my field of specialty. In his book *Financial Forensics Body of Knowledge* (Wiley 2012), Darrell Dorrell defines forensic accounting as the "art and science of investigating people and money" (p. 6). This definition is simple but accurate. The other professionals listed above are perfectly capable of performing work in their areas of expertise. Nevertheless, the focus of this book will remain on the forensic accountant who works exclusively in the areas of litigation and fraud. Throughout this book I will refer to the professional doing a lifestyle analysis in a divorce as a forensic accountant, financial expert, or financial analyst, using the terms interchangeably.

What is so special about a forensic accountant? Accountants providing traditional services focus on things like income tax return preparation, financial statement preparation, reviews and audits of financial statements, and general financial consulting. Forensic accounting builds on many of the core concepts and skills used in providing traditional accounting services but also requires effective use of investigative techniques to sort out complicated situations involving numbers. It is a specialty requiring an additional set of skills and investigative intuition.

Simply put, not every accountant can effectively provide forensic services. Traditional accountants and their firms are eager to provide forensic services, but it is important for the attorney to look into the professional's level of experience in litigation and forensic work to be certain that he or she is qualified for the engagement.

One of the most important considerations in choosing a financial professional to assist with a family law case is his or her qualifications. Although family law cases fall under state laws, the Federal Rules of Evidence are instructive in evaluating the qualifications. Some states have adopted the Federal Rules of Evidence as they relate to expert witnesses or use variations strikingly similar to the federal rules.

Rule 702, Testimony by Expert Witnesses, of the Federal Rules of Evidence reads:

> A witness who is qualified as an expert by knowledge, skill, experience, training, or education may testify in the form of an opinion or otherwise if:
> (a) the expert's scientific, technical, or other specialized knowledge will help the trier of fact to understand the evidence or to determine a fact in issue;
> (b) the testimony is based on sufficient facts or data;
> (c) the testimony is the product of reliable principles and methods; and
> (d) the expert has reliably applied the principles and methods to the facts of the case.

The judge in the divorce case will decide if the financial expert meets these qualifications and is therefore permitted to testify as an expert witness.

A U.S. Supreme Court decision in *Daubert v. Merrell Dow Pharmaceuticals, Inc.*, 509 U.S. 579 (1993), is also instructive when evaluating a financial professional's qualifications. In *Daubert*, the Supreme Court designated the trial judge as the gatekeeper for deciding whether an expert used reliable methodology. The judge applies the following factors in deciding the admissibility of the expert's testimony:

(a) Whether the theory or technique has been tested or can be tested,
(b) Whether the theory has been subjected to peer review and publication,
(c) Whether there is a known or potential error rate of the theory or technique,
(d) Whether the theory has general acceptance by the relevant scientific community.

In lay terms, the question is whether the expert used recognized methodology in coming to his or her conclusions. Has the forensic accountant made the calculations in a way that other forensic accountants would agree is valid?

It is important for an expert witness to be aware of Rule 702 and *Daubert* if the court in which he or she is testifying adheres to the Federal Rules of Evidence. In the event that the court instead relies on state rules, the witness should familiarize himself or herself with the specific rules that will apply to his or her expert witness testimony.

Regardless of whether the court evaluates an expert witness under federal or state rules of evidence, the expert's education, training, and certifications will be examined during the qualifications phase. This may include evaluation of the expert's curriculum vitae (CV) outlining his or her education, credentials, work history, and relevant experience. Testimony may be taken from the expert to determine whether he or she has sufficient knowledge and experience in the area in which he or she is providing opinions.

In order for the expert to provide value to the case at the trial, he or she must be deemed an expert by the court. Anyone could call himself or herself an expert, but unless the court says someone is an expert in the case at hand, the word *expert* means nothing. Thus, the qualifications phase is extremely important. The expert must be adept at demonstrating his or her training, skills, and experience and how they are relevant to the case at hand.

One important area often evaluated by the court is the credentials of the financial expert. A forensic accountant can possess a variety of certifications. It is important to evaluate these certificates and credentials to determine the substance behind them.

The most widely respected credentials in the field of forensic accounting include the following:

- Certified Public Accountant (CPA)—Most forensic accountants serving as expert witnesses have a CPA license. The CPA license is granted by each state after the candidate successfully completes a very difficult examination and practice requirements. In addition, most states require ongoing continuing education to maintain the license. The CPA license is a broad credential signifying expertise in accounting in general. It is not necessary for a forensic accountant to have a CPA license in a state in which he or she is testifying. However, a CPA license from any state will demonstrate that the expert has a certain level of skill in accounting matters.
- Certified in Financial Forensics (CFF)—This credential is offered by the American Institute of Certified Public Accountants (AICPA), the national organization open to CPAs. The credential is earned by passing an exam and meeting certain experience requirements. Annual continuing education is required to maintain the credential. The CFF designation indicates knowledge and experience related to fraud, forensic accounting, and litigation.
- Certified Fraud Examiner (CFE)—The CFE credential is awarded by the Association of Certified Fraud Examiners (ACFE), the largest antifraud organization in the world. It is earned by passing an exam and meeting experience requirements, and it requires annual continuing education credits. The CFE designation speaks to knowledge and experience in the areas of fraud and litigation.
- Master Analyst in Financial Forensics (MAFF)—The MAFF designation is awarded by the National Association of Certified Valuators and

Analysts (NACVA) to signify mastery of financial forensics techniques and concepts. The credential is earned upon meeting education and experience requirements and passing an exam.

- Certified Valuation Analyst (CVA)—The NACVA offers this designation to professionals who pass an examination and meet certain experience requirements. Continuing education is required each year to maintain the certification. The CVA credential indicates knowledge and experience in completing business valuations.
- Accredited in Business Valuation (ABV)—The AICPA offers the ABV credential to any qualified finance professional. Previously it was offered only to CPAs, but recently it was opened to other financial professionals who provide business valuations. Eligible professionals must meet certain requirements related to business valuation education and work and must pass an exam.
- Certified Financial Planner (CFP)—The CFP designation is issued by the Certified Financial Planner Board of Standards (CFP Board) to professionals who pass an examination and complete experience requirements. Annual continuing education is required to maintain the certification. The CFP credential signifies expertise in the area of financial planning, and CFPs may be qualified to render opinions related to pensions and investments.
- Chartered Financial Analyst (CFA)—A professional can obtain the CFA credential from the CFA Institute by completing an examination and meeting experience requirements. Annual continuing education is required to maintain the credential. The CFA designation indicates knowledge in investment analysis.

Individuals working in the areas of fraud, litigation, and business valuations may possess many other credentials; however, the substance behind these credentials should be carefully evaluated. Some certifications have few requirements, as holders of one or more of the certifications listed here may automatically qualify. Other certifications are really just marketing tools for the professionals. Many of the "credentials" offered today afford inadequate quality control, so those certifications mean little related to the expertise of a financial professional.

Why might an attorney want to use a professional with a "lesser" credential? Maybe the client cannot afford to hire a very qualified expert to do the financial analysis but still needs an unbiased third party to provide an analysis for the court. In this case, the attorney may select a professional with a credential other than the ones above.

Some of the other considerations the attorney may take into account when choosing a financial expert witness include:

- How the expert's credentials enhance this specific case
- The expert's strengths and weaknesses in these matters
- How this expert compares to or stands out from other forensic accountants
- Professional writing done by the expert (articles and books)
- Seminars presented by the forensic accountant
- How many times the financial expert has testified at deposition and trial
- Whether the expert's testimony has ever been limited by a court
- If a business is involved, experience in its industry
- Any conflicts of interest related to the parties and the attorneys
- Whether the expert can meet the deadlines set forth in the case

These points may speak to the strength of the financial expert's experience and how qualified her or she may appear.

It is important to inquire into whether an expert has been disqualified or had his or her testimony limited in any prior case. Experts who testify routinely may have been subject to *Daubert* challenges numerous times. Therefore, it is critical to find out whether the expert's testimony was ever limited or excluded and why. Remember that it is possible the expert did nothing wrong but the testimony was limited due to unique issues of the case, conduct of the client, or other factors outside the expert's control.

Family law attorney Miles Mason provides the following tips for discovering whether an expert was previously disqualified in a case:

There are a number of ways to determine whether an expert witness has been disqualified in a previous case or has had testimony limited by the trier of fact. Check Google, case law research, and the Daubert

Tracker. The Daubert Tracker is a national database of appellate opinions where you can search cases by name. It is currently free to AICPA Forensic and Valuation Services Section members. Another good old-fashioned way is to ask around. Call competing expert witnesses. Call well-known family law attorneys likely to have opposed that witness. See if the gossip mill can turn up anything.

Don't overplay your hand. Keep in mind that if an expert witness had some part of their testimony excluded, it could have just resulted from an overly exuberant trial attorney trying to push something past its logical course. Or, the trial judge might have simply wanted to limit testimony to quicken the pace of a lengthy hearing.

If the opposing expert has been disqualified, the family lawyer needs as many of the details as possible before digging in. Copy of the transcript? Findings of fact? Formal ruling on a motion in limine? Find out what's what. If a financial expert witness has been disqualified at a trial, the reason why could be very important. For example, if an expert witness was disclosed past the expert witness disclosure deadline in a scheduling order, that is not the expert's fault. It was the client's trial attorney's fault. But, if a financial expert was proffered as an expert witness to calculate the estimated value of a pension interest and the expert failed to request the pension's summary plan description and misinterpreted the meaning of a financial figure in the annual benefits statement, that mistake is a big one. That can be argued to be a terrible error in judgment. Depending on the issue at hand, evidence of shoddy work can be devastating in all future testimonies (if there are any).

Professional Standards

Each credentialing body has its own set of professional standards to which members must adhere. The AICPA's standards are the most common standards applicable to forensic accountants. Under Rule 201, General Standards, the professional should only accept engagements he or she can complete with competence. This means the forensic accountant should know what specific skills or knowledge are necessary for an engagement and should accept that engagement only if he or she (or the firm) possesses the requisite skills and knowledge.

Rule 201 also specifies that the accountant must use due professional care in completing engagements, must properly plan and supervise the engagement, and must have sufficient relevant data to support the conclusions reached during the engagement. An expert should be able to articulate how the professionals performing services during the course of the engagement are competent to do those tasks and how they were supervised to ensure a quality work product.

Sufficient relevant data can become a sticking point in forensic accounting engagements. If documents are missing or if estimates need to be made, the financial expert must carefully consider whether there was sufficient data to come to a reasonable conclusion in the engagement.

Additional guidance on the performance of family law engagements may be found in the following AICPA special reports and practice aids:

- Litigation Services and Applicable Professional Standards—AICPA Consulting Services Special Report
- Communicating in Litigation Services: Reports—AICPA Practice Aid
- Engagement Letters for Litigation Services—AICPA Practice Aid
- Forensic Accounting—Fraud Investigations—AICPA Practice Aid
- Serving as an Expert Witness or Consultant—AICPA Practice Aid, 2nd Edition
- Introduction to Civil Litigation—AICPA Practice Aid, 2nd Edition
- A CPA's Guide to Family Law Services—AICPA Practice Aid, 2nd Edition

Conflicts of Interest

The family law attorney should consider whether a forensic accountant has any actual or perceived conflicts of interest in the engagement. This is important because the professional may not be considered credible if there is an apparent bias or conflict of interest. One example of a potential conflict of interest is previously providing professional services for either spouse or for a business owned by or involving either spouse.

A previous engagement with the attorney will not constitute a per se conflict of interest. However, an expert witness may appear to be biased if he or she has performed numerous engagements for the retaining attorney. A lengthy financial relationship between the forensic accountant and the attorney does not necessarily mean that the expert lacks objectivity, but the issue may arise in court and may affect the perception of credibility.

It is important for the financial expert to be independent during the engagement. That is, he or she should have no financial interest in the outcome of the divorce proceedings. Of course, the expert has a financial interest of sorts, as he or she is compensated by the spouses for work performed. However, it is understood that professionals ought to be paid for their services, and receiving fair compensation for services performed does not impair the expert's independence.

Consulting Versus Testifying

A financial professional can fill two distinct roles in family law cases. He or she can be a consultant who provides analysis and opinions privately to the attorney and client. In this case, the consulting expert's work and conclusions are not intended to be presented in court but are intended to be advisory. The other role is that of a testifying expert, alternately called an expert witness. The testifying expert must be disclosed in the event that the case goes to trial.

The services of a consulting expert may include any of the following:

- Explaining financial topics to the attorney and client
- Providing opinions and advice on financial matters, including the value of assets and liabilities, the taxability of settlement scenarios, and the strengths and weaknesses of the financial portion of the case
- Helping to develop a litigation strategy
- Devising a strategy for presenting financial issues to the court

- Evaluating a testifying expert's work as a "second set of eyes," which may help identify weaknesses or opportunities in the testifying expert's work
- Scrutinizing the work of a financial neutral appointed in the divorce
- Evaluating the work of a financial expert retained by the opposing party to find deficiencies in the work
- Helping the attorney prepare for depositions that may include financial questions

The work of the consulting expert, including his or her notes, communications, calculations, e-mails, letters, and other documentation, is typically protected as attorney work product. Accordingly, the knowledge, opinions, and files of the accountant are not discoverable by the opposing party.

However, it is important to recognize that the consulting expert could later become a testifying expert. In that case, the materials developed during the consultation process will likely become discoverable. Thus, the consultant should carefully maintain his or her files in the event that the work product is someday discoverable, even if this possibility is remote.

A forensic accountant retained as a testifying expert may do many of the same things as the consulting expert. Opinions on the value of assets or liabilities, analysis of the tax impact of various settlement scenarios, calculation of the "lifestyle" of the divorcing parties, or evaluation of the financial issues in the case may be done. In addition, the expert witness may be required to testify in depositions or at trials, explaining his or her work, file materials, opinions, and conclusions. Remember that the file of the testifying expert will be discoverable.

As discussed previously, the objectivity of the testifying expert will be carefully scrutinized. The expert witness is expected to evaluate evidence and come to independent conclusions that are not biased. The witness must be careful to avoid the appearance of being a "hired gun" in the case.

Reasons for Hiring an Expert

Some family law attorneys are reluctant to retain forensic accountants. Money may be a factor, but sometimes the need for an outside expert is not clear. Even though law firms may have paralegals or attorneys on staff who are very knowledgeable about financial issues, the outside forensic accountant offers the following advantages:

- Experience in financial investigations means the work can be completed quicker and more efficiently. The results are often presented better because experts regularly present their results in court and they are used to making financial matters understandable for non-accountants. It is often more cost-effective to have a forensic accountant perform the preliminary work on the numbers even though a paralegal or legal assistant may have a much lower billing rate. The expert's familiarity with numbers leads to efficiencies and often a lower overall cost.
- An outside expert can testify, whereas law firm personnel cannot. Even though the family lawyer might not intend for the case to go to trial, it is always a possibility; therefore, it pays to have a financial professional who could testify if necessary.
- An outside expert is generally perceived as more objective. Ethical forensic accountants attempt to be independent and objective in their opinions, which bolsters the credibility of the calculations.
- Forensic accountants have experience finding red flags and issues. Their analysis is often more thorough, and their ability to spot problems is often more developed. This can be invaluable for finding red flags and issues that were previously unknown.
- Having a strong financial expert on your team could push the case toward resolution. The other side knows you are serious about sorting out the financial issues and finding details relevant to your client's case. There is power in having a strong team and being prepared.

Accountants and Attorneys Working Together

The expert's assistance with the discovery process can be invaluable to the family law attorney. By virtue of the expert's familiarity with personal and business financial documents, the financial expert can play an important role in the discovery process. He or she can help with the following:

- Determining which documents should be requested or subpoenaed
- Identifying the individuals or companies most likely to possess those documents
- Drafting discovery requests, using the common names of the financial documents in conjunction with descriptions that may be important in the event that the person or company uses a different name for the documents or reports
- Evaluating documents produced in discovery to determine if they are responsive to the requests or subpoenas
- Drafting follow-up requests either to reiterate or reword the original requests or to create additional requests or demands
- Helping with wording for motions to compel financial discovery
- Explaining the documents and data to the attorneys
- Assisting with the preparation for depositions of individuals who have financial information relevant to the family law case
- Attending depositions of parties with financial information to provide the attorney with suggested lines of questioning

The forensic accountant may also assist the family lawyer with the development of strategy for the financial portion of the case. The expert's financial and business experience may aid the attorney in understanding and litigating the issues related to the finances of the family.

It is important that the financial expert not be afraid to point out weaknesses and errors in the financial case, perhaps guiding the attorney to a better understanding of the financial issues and an alternative, more viable approach. For example, the client may have calculated historical expenditures including certain items that may not be recurring. The expert can identify those items, point out the fact that such expenses will not be incurred in the future, and adjust the expense budget accordingly. The attorney and client retain the financial expert presumably because of financial knowledge. It is up to the expert to be proactive in helping the attorney understand the issues and know early on about potential roadblocks in the case.

The Lifestyle Analysis

This book focuses solely on the lifestyle analysis in the family law case, although other services from a financial professional may also be needed in a case. The financial goal in a divorce is an equitable arrangement in which the assets and liabilities are divided and the future income is potentially shared via support orders. The lifestyle analysis is the process of tabulating and analyzing the income and expenses of the parties. The lifestyle analysis is then used to determine the standard of living of the parties, which will influence support calculations, and possibly property division.

Calculating the lifestyle of the spouses prior to separation can provide insight into the lifestyle the married couple enjoyed and the cost of that lifestyle, as well as the income that was or is required to fund the lifestyle of the married couple. The results may be used to prove a spouse's financial needs following divorce. In other words, a detailed analysis of the spending during the marriage can be the basis to calculate the funding the spouse needs to maintain a similar lifestyle after divorce.

The lifestyle analysis may also help confirm or refute income claims made by a spouse. If a spouse has declared income that is well below the cost of the lifestyle he or she is leading, the lifestyle analysis may suggest that undisclosed sources of income exist. It may also help identify previously undisclosed assets, which may have a substantial impact on the property division.

Investigating historical income and expenses is a process of working backward from the present time to see how the couple achieved their current financial status. For each financial transaction in which a party is involved, there are multiple pieces of documentation and evidence. Part of the forensic analysis may be trying to locate multiple sources of evidence that help prove the flow of funds. This is particularly true if a document or representation may be unreliable. When confirming or refuting income claims made by a spouse, searching for alternative sources of income can help clarify the issue.

The lifestyle analysis is typically used to sort out the numbers post-separation, but it may also be used to evaluate the finances of each party at the time of a prenuptial agreement. If a party did not make a full and accurate disclosure prior to the signing of the premarital agreement, the spouse may attempt to have the agreement set aside. A prenuptial agreement can also be instrumental in the forensic accountant's work post-separation, as it provides a point at which to start tracing funds or assets.

Determining Support

The lifestyle analysis can be a key component in the determination of support, including both spousal support (also called alimony or maintenance) and child support.

The following four types of spousal support are typical in divorces:

- Temporary support is paid on a short-term basis. It may also be called rehabilitative support. This type of spousal support is awarded for a limited period of time, as the recipient is expected to be working toward becoming self-sufficient. It is typical to award temporary support when a spouse is returning to school, receiving job training, or working on career development. Usually temporary support is modifiable if there is a change in circumstances.
- Long-term spousal support can also be called permanent support and is generally intended to be paid to the spouse for the remainder of his or her life. In addition to terminating upon death, permanent support may also be terminated if the spouse remarries or has a change in circumstances. A change in circumstances could also cause the amount of permanent support to be modified. Common reasons to modify permanent support include significant health issues, changes in income (for either of the parties), or changes in need.
- Reimbursement support is meant to compensate the recipient for expenses paid during the marriage. For example, if one spouse used nonmarital funds to put the other spouse through medical school, the

divorce may include reimbursement support for the cost of the education. Reimbursement support could also cover things like real estate taxes on separate property paid with marital funds.

- Lump sum support is paid as a specific amount up front. This type of support generally arises out of a settlement agreement during a divorce. It may be helpful to one or both of the parties because it brings certainty to the situation right away.

Spousal support and child support can be calculated using a number of different factors, including:

- The actual earnings of each person, including wages, investment income, and other sources of income (retirement, disability, trusts, etc.)
- Present earning capacity of each party, both independently and relatively
- Future earning capacity of the parties
- The value of the assets divided and the ability of those assets to produce income
- The cash flow of each party
- The length of the marriage or relationship
- The ages of the individuals
- The needs of the spouses or parties and the needs of the children
- The ability of the parties to pay support
- The standard of living (or lifestyle) established during the marriage
- Impairment of earning capacity due to devoting time to domestic duties, delaying education or employment, forgoing career opportunities during the marriage, and the like
- Contributions to the other party's education, training, or career
- The effect that parenting arrangements may have on a party's ability to seek or maintain employment
- Income taxes that will be incurred by each party
- Short-term and long-term expenses expected to be incurred
- Valid agreements of the parties
- Other factors that a court finds to be just and equitable under the circumstances

Most of these factors have a great deal of "gray area." Reasonable people can disagree on how to calculate them or how significant a role they should play in the calculation of support. Consider, for example, the following issues:

- Actual earnings—What should be included or excluded from this calculation? Are there certain types of earnings that are nonrecurring or so uncertain as to make it unfair to include them in a calculation of ongoing earnings?
- Earning capacity—What is the spouse's true earning capacity? What if the spouse cannot find employment within his or her area of expertise? What if the spouse no longer wishes to work in the area of expertise? What if the spouse needs or wants to work less than full-time? What if the spouse quits a job to start a business, and that business will not create income for a period of time? What if a spouse decides to take early retirement?
- Value of assets divided—The parties may disagree on the value of assets being divided, as well as how much income will be derived from those assets in the future. They may also disagree on whether a spouse should sell an asset to generate funds. The sale of assets to fund current expenses could have a dramatic long-term impact, particularly for a spouse who does not have the ability to generate income or save additional money for future needs.
- Cash flow—Cash received from work and business activities is not necessarily the same thing as income from those activities. For example, income-producing real estate often has higher cash flow than the income reported on a tax return. How heavily should the cash flow be considered? Is it more or less indicative of the need for support or the ability to pay than some other factor?
- Needs of parties—What is truly "needed" by the parties following the divorce? Should the post-divorce lifestyle include all of the things that were enjoyed during the marriage? Were portions of the lifestyle "excessive"? If so, should they not be considered a true need? What if the parties lived very frugally during the marriage? Should the spouses be required to continue to live in a frugal fashion?

- Ability to pay—Which items of income or cash flow should be included when calculating a spouse's ability to pay? Should certain funds or earnings be excluded? What if certain income is used to start or grow a business venture? If the earnings invested into a business are excluded from support calculations, should the future earnings from that business venture be included in support calculations at some point? Should a spouse be allowed to save certain funds, rather than have them considered income on which support is calculated?
- Standard of living—Jurisdictions vary regarding how standard of living is defined. Chapter 2 will discuss this in detail.
- Impairment of earning capacity—How impaired is the earning capacity? Whose fault is the impairment, and should this affect support calculations? How can we fairly estimate what the earning capacity could have been without the impairment or what it will be in the future?
- Contributions—How do we value and weight the contributions of one party to the other party's career?
- Short-term and long-term expenses—Which expenses should be considered, and how heavily should they be weighted? Should any expenses be excluded because they are discretionary?

Of course, states vary in the factors to be considered regarding support or maintenance. For example, the Illinois Marriage and Dissolution of Marriage Act, Section 504, currently states that temporary or permanent maintenance will be paid based on a consideration of the following relevant factors:

1. the income and property of each party, including marital property apportioned and non-marital property assigned to the party seeking maintenance as well as all financial obligations imposed on the parties as a result of the dissolution of marriage;
2. the needs of each party;
3. the realistic present and future earning capacity of each party;
4. any impairment of the present and future earning capacity of the party seeking maintenance due to that party devoting time to domestic duties or having forgone or delayed education, training, employment, or career opportunities due to the marriage;

5. any impairment of the realistic present or future earning capacity of the party against whom maintenance is sought;
6. the time necessary to enable the party seeking maintenance to acquire appropriate education, training, and employment, and whether that party is able to support himself or herself through appropriate employment;
>   6.1. the effect of any parental responsibility arrangements and its effect on a party's ability to seek or maintain employment;
7. the standard of living established during the marriage;
8. the duration of the marriage;
9. the age, health, station, occupation, amount and sources of income, vocational skills, employability, estate, liabilities, and the needs of each of the parties;
10. all sources of public and private income including, without limitation, disability and retirement income;
11. the tax consequences to each party;
12. contributions and services by the party seeking maintenance to the education, training, career or career potential, or license of the other spouse;
13. any valid agreement of the parties; and
14. any other factor that the court expressly finds to be just and equitable.

The list of factors to be considered in support calculations provided earlier in this chapter is a bit more generic, whereas the list of factors from Illinois gets a bit more specific. Be aware that the guidance in state law can and does change routinely. The Illinois statute had substantive changes between the first and second editions of this book.

Post-divorce budgets play a huge role in determining spousal support and child support. One of the most basic uses of a lifestyle analysis is creating budgets, especially for parties with very high incomes. By analyzing historical expenditures of the parties, a more precise budget for future expenses can be created. This is not simply a matter of tabulating historical spending. The forensic accountant needs to be skilled in spotting irregularities in the numbers that may suggest missing documents, expenses that haven't been accounted for, or other problems with the figures. Certain adjustments also may need to be made to past expenses to include or eliminate certain items. The financial expert should develop a basis for those adjustments and be ready to articulate it.

For example, consider a case in which the parties were living rent-free in a residence owned by the wife's parents during the marriage. Following the separation, one or both of the parties may need to pay for housing, and this must be added to the budget. Conversely, consider a case in which the parties had a large expense for an anniversary party for themselves. Since they will be divorced, this expense will not occur again in the future, so it should likely be removed from the budget. A budget developed using only historical expenses without adjustments for items like these would be inaccurate in estimating future spending.

Evaluating historical spending and creating budgets is covered in detail in Chapter 8, where we discuss considerations in assessing these figures.

Tax Law Changes

The Tax Cuts and Jobs Act of 2017 (TCJA) made significant changes to federal income tax filings for individuals. The provision relevant to the material in this book relates to how spousal support payments are treated for tax purposes. For divorce or separation instruments executed before 2019, the payer of spousal support deducts the payments from his or her income, and the recipient includes the payments in his or her taxable income.

Divorce or separation instruments executed after December 31, 2018 have a different set of rules. Payment of spousal support is not deductible by the payer, and the recipient of the support payments does not include them in taxable income. Since the payer of spousal support is most often the party with higher earnings (and therefore sometimes a higher tax rate), the law change effectively increases the total tax burden of the couple.

This may be seen as a win for the party receiving spousal support. The recipient spouse receives the income tax-free, which seems to be a benefit. But the reality is that he or she will likely receive less money each month to factor in the tax impact of this change.

Separate Property

Jurisdictions vary in their definitions of separate property and how a party must prove or document the separateness of the property. Regardless of a jurisdiction's rules, a lifestyle analysis can be used to trace assets, how those assets were acquired, the source of funds used to acquire the assets, whether the assets were maintained separately during the marriage, and the use of the proceeds of sales of the assets. The lifestyle analysis can be instrumental in proving (or disproving) that an asset was acquired with separate funds and was kept separate throughout the duration of the marriage. In Chapter 10, we cover the issue of separate property in more detail.

Hidden Income

The lifestyle analysis can be used to uncover hidden sources of income. In Chapter 9, we discuss how income is defined and a number of the common complications that can arise in calculating it. We also discuss common ways that sources of income are hidden and commonly used methods to uncover them.

When income is difficult or impossible to calculate because documents are not being produced or financial information is being obscured, a lifestyle analysis may be used circumstantially to prove the level of income of a party. If the level of spending of that party can be proven or reasonably estimated, an inference can be made that sufficient income exists to fund that spending.

Naturally, the other side of the case will likely challenge the lifestyle analysis and say the income calculated is speculative. The goal is to gather as much information and evidence as possible to make reasonable calculations and estimates. Remember that these calculations would not be necessary if the spouse was forthcoming with documentation and disclosures. While estimates and circumstantial evidence of income are not ideal, sometimes they are the only alternative in a case in which a party is concealing information.

Hidden Assets

The lifestyle analysis can also be used to uncover hidden assets. It is often difficult to find assets around the world with a "wild goose chase" by a private investigator, especially if the spouse is adept at hiding things. Tracing funds can sometimes uncover those assets, however. Undisclosed assets can be found because of a transfer of money or the payment of a bill that indicates the existence of an asset. We discuss hidden assets in detail in Chapter 10, including how to identify and classify assets, methods used to hide assets, and techniques used to uncover hidden assets.

Chapter 2

Standard of Living

An area of divorce financial analysis of great interest to attorneys and accountants is the standard of living, both during and after the marriage. Jurisdictions have varying factors that come into play when determining the standard of living during the marriage. The attorney must be familiar with local rules. However, this chapter details some of the most important factors to be considered in analyzing the standard of living of spouses.

To be clear, the discussion of standard of living in this chapter is simply the author's viewpoint on the most important factors. This viewpoint was developed after consulting on the issue of lifestyle in family law cases in various states. The family lawyer's local rules will take precedence; however, the factors discussed here may be presented to the court for consideration. The more familiar the family law attorney is with these issues, the better the attorney may be able to present the position and the more convincing the argument may be for the court to consider additional factors.

Introduction to Standard of Living

For the purpose of calculating alimony, courts consider a variety of factors, and the standard of living established during the marriage is included in that analysis. It is important to consider not only the standard of living during the marriage but also whether the parties can maintain a reasonably comparable standard of living following the divorce. In many cases, the same standard of living cannot be maintained because there is not enough income to maintain two households of comparable quality to the marital household.

In some cases, however, it may be possible to maintain the standard of living established during the marriage, particularly if the family was living below its means or had very high income. If the family was not spending all that it earned on the lifestyle, it may be possible to fully fund two comparable households after the divorce. There may even be enough earnings to fund savings, which could be a part of the standard of living too.

Attorneys and financial experts sometimes argue that historical expenditures of the family (without any adjustments whatsoever) are the sole basis on which the standard of living should be established. This approach is upheld by courts in some cases, but often it is not a good way to calculate the standard of living because unusual things happen before and after divorce. The only way to properly account for those unusual situations is through adjustments to the historical expenditures.

Standard of living encompasses more than just historical figures. The five most important factors that should affect the calculation of the standard of living are:

- Earned and unearned income
- Funding sources for the lifestyle
- Actual historical expenditures
- Existence of unusual, nonrecurring expenses
- Reasonable needs in the future

Earned and Unearned Income

Lifestyle is not simply a measure of the past, present, and future spending of the parties jointly and individually. It requires an analysis of the funds available to pay for this lifestyle, and earned and unearned income usually generates those funds.

Earned income generally includes income generated by working or providing personal services such as:

- Wages, salaries, tips, commissions, bonuses, and other taxable employee pay

- Net earnings from self-employment, including entities established as sole proprietorships, partnerships, corporations, LLCs, or some other form of business
- Royalties, earnings under endorsement deals, and other unusual forms of income

Unearned income generally includes any earnings that do not originate from a spouse's job or active business venture such as:

- Income from investments in which neither spouse actively works or participates, such as interest and dividends from savings accounts, investment accounts, or stock ownership in public companies
- Capital gains from the sale of investments
- Income from trusts
- Income from estates
- Inheritances
- Income from real estate ventures in which neither spouse actively works or participates
- Retirement earnings such as annuities, pensions, or Social Security
- Unemployment or workers' compensation income
- Settlements and awards
- Proceeds of life insurance policies
- Prizes or lottery winnings

Income from investments is often hotly debated in divorces, especially when the investments and related gains are substantial. One issue is whether assets should be invested differently, potentially to increase or maximize the earnings from those investments. Another issue is whether investments should be liquidated for distribution to the spouses or to fund purchases, educations, and other substantial expenses. Additionally, it is not uncommon for spouses to dispute how income or losses from investments should be apportioned to the individuals.

Capital gains income from investments can be a contentious area as well. Even though capital gains are considered income for income tax purposes, parties to a divorce may argue that they are not income, but a liquidation of assets. It is important to evaluate what happened with the asset leading up to the sale of it. For example, if the asset is a rental property for which depreciation and other expenses reduced the income available for support in prior years, then the sale of the asset may need to be included in income at the time of sale to remain consistent. If the expenses related to the asset reduced income in previous years, then the income from the asset's sale should increase income in the current year.

It is important to know if the capital gains income was actually received by the parties or whether it was rolled into another investment. Taxpayers can use like-kind exchange rules to defer paying taxes on capital gains on real estate if they identify and purchase like-kind property. This is sometimes called a section 1031 exchange, as the rules are contained in Section 1031 of the Internal Revenue Code. While a taxpayer may not receive cash in hand for the capital gains realized on the sold real estate, the gain still existed and was used to obtain a better asset. The value of the newly acquired asset must be considered.

Historical earned and unearned income must be evaluated to determine whether the income is predictable or follows some sort of pattern. The history will be used to project future earnings, along with other important information such as the ability of the spouses to maintain employment and earnings or to continue to generate investment returns. Support may be set based on projected earnings, but if earnings fluctuate, it may be necessary to return to court to reconcile the amount of support due based on actual earnings.

Funding Sources for the Lifestyle

An important lifestyle consideration is the source of funding. Many families fund their lifestyle with one source of income, earned from work. Other families have multiple sources of income that may include investments, trusts, debt, gifts, liquidation of assets, or other sources.

The funding sources matter when examining the lifestyle and determining the standard of living for a number of reasons:

- The sources may not be guaranteed in the future.
- The sources may be exhausted at some point in the future.

- It may not be reasonable to require the use of the sources to fund the lifestyle.

For example, if the wage income of the parties did not fully fund the lifestyle during the marriage, and the parties incurred debt to maintain the lifestyle, the court may be reluctant to order that the same lifestyle be maintained after the divorce. Courts often will not require one or both of the spouses to incur debt to maintain a lifestyle that arguably is (and was) beyond the means of the spouses. Borrowing to fund the family's lifestyle is also not sustainable. If spending continuously outpaces income, debt cannot be accumulated indefinitely.

Issues may also arise when expenses are funded by trusts, inheritances, gifts, or other sources that may not guarantee funding in the future. Such sources of funds are generally not unlimited, so the availability of those sources in the future is often questionable. For example, if assets have been liquidated to fund the family's lifestyle, an argument can be made that liquidating assets is not a sustainable source of funding. Eventually there will be no assets left to sell.

A lifestyle funded in part or full by gifts or loans from friends or family is problematic as well. For example, consider a residence owned by the family of one of the spouses. The family allowed the spouses to live in the home rent-free for the duration of the marriage. This is arguably a funding source, as the family is providing the value of the residence. This funding could stop at any time, and that possibility must be considered when evaluating the standard of living.

Remember that the property divided in a divorce may include a funding source. If the spouse receives investments or other property that produces income or cash flow, this will fund the lifestyle in part or full. The spouse's need for support should be adjusted accordingly so as not to provide the spouse with a duplicate benefit in the divorce.

Actual Historical Expenditures

Often, it is argued that support must be paid in an amount that will allow the recipient to live a lifestyle reasonably comparable to the one enjoyed during the marriage. The lifestyle during the marriage is determined by analyzing the family's historical expenditures. The lifestyle analysis aimed at evaluating historical expenditures is discussed in detail in Chapters 7 and 8.

Expenditures should be categorized and may also be allocated based on the family member benefitting from the expenditures. For example, expenses relating to children may be segregated to address those expenses separately from the issues of property division or spousal support.

The spending of each spouse may be critically analyzed not only to categorize the spending but also to determine whether the spending was reasonable. Some attorneys argue that whether the spending was reasonable or outrageous is irrelevant; the fact that the spending occurred is enough to establish the standard of living. Other attorneys argue that over-the-top spending during the marriage should not set a precedent for the lifestyle after the divorce. It may be argued that extreme spending should not have occurred during the marriage and support should be adjusted downward to address excessive spending.

It is easy to see how this can be a contentious issue, as many marital problems have their origins in arguments about money. The rules in state courts often do not provide full clarity on the issue of historical spending. Judges have a certain degree of latitude in evaluating the lifestyle, which opens the door to arguments for and against using historical expenditures as a basis for calculating the standard of living.

In addition to the issues discussed so far, the spending of the parties may be evaluated to determine if it was for a marital or nonmarital purpose. Expenditures that were kept secret from a spouse or made without the spouse's approval may require further scrutiny. For example, expenses related to a mistress or drug activity may be considered nonmarital and excluded from the lifestyle analysis accordingly. Excluded items may encompass those things that involved illegal, dishonest, fraudulent, or immoral behavior and provided no benefit to the family.

Existence of Unusual, Nonrecurring Expenses

Expenses that are not expected to recur should be excluded from the marital lifestyle. The rationale is simple: If an expense will not recur, either due to the end of the marriage or some other relevant factor, it is not part of the lifestyle that must be funded post-divorce.

Examples of items that should be excluded from the marital lifestyle could include:

- Large spousal gifts such as jewelry—The spouses will presumably not give one another gifts after the marriage ends, so gifts to each other are not part of the post-divorce lifestyle.
- Anniversary trips or parties—Because the marriage is ending, any expenditures related to the anniversary of the spouses should be excluded from the lifestyle.
- Funding for extended family—The partial or full support of extended family members may need to be excluded from lifestyle. For example, suppose the married couple pays the medical expenses of the wife's parents for a period of ten years during the marriage. These expenses are likely to be excluded from the standard of living as the parties would not be forced to pay such things post-divorce.

Many expenditures could fall into this gray area, and those expenditures will have to be evaluated individually. What may be considered nonrecurring for one couple may be recurring for another couple.

Certain capital expenditures made by the family may need to be removed from the calculation of the standard of living. For example, if the family purchased household furnishings and the spouse is entitled to a share of that furniture, then funds might not be allocated for furniture when calculating the standard of living. To allocate funds for furniture in this case may double-count the item. However, funds may need to be budgeted for future replacement of that furniture.

Purchases of larger items such as automobiles, boats, and residences may also need to be adjusted when calculating the standard of living. For example, it may be necessary to determine how long (on average) the family used a vehicle before replacing it, and that information may be used to adjust lifestyle analysis to reflect "normal" expenditures for vehicles.

Items representing dissipation or marital waste should not be included in the lifestyle. Spending for non-marital purposes is not part of the marital lifestyle. What is commonly considered dissipation? Common items included in dissipation claims are affairs, strip clubs, prostitutes, gambling, drugs, or other illegal activity. Varying items could be considered dissipation depending on the circumstances and whether the spouse knew about them and/or approved of using marital funds for them. Some of the more common items that fall in this gray area may include stock trading losses, expenditures on eccentric hobbies, investments in speculative businesses or unusual activities, or risky loans (especially to related parties).

Dissipation claims can be difficult to prove, as there is often not much of a paper trail documenting the expenditures. Often cash is used for items that may be considered dissipation, specifically because cash leaves no paper trail. How does one prove that an expensive dinner out was with a mistress? This is a difficult thing to prove, although social media activity can sometimes help provide some clarity.

In one case, the husband openly had a girlfriend whom he supported with an apartment, a car, clothing, jewelry, vacations, and dinners. The spending on the apartment and car was obvious, but it was difficult to pinpoint the other expenditures. The girlfriend had a social media account on which she posted pictures at restaurants and stores, flaunting what she was buying. Each Instagram picture had a date and was often tagged with a location. Hundreds of publicly available pictures were compared to credit card bills, leading to a dissipation claim of more than $300,000. This was an unusual situation as social media information like this is not often available, but it proves that it is possible to use social media to support a dissipation claim.

The difficulty in proving dissipation and quantifying the economic impact should not dissuade counsel from pursuing a valid claim. If enough money is at stake, it may be a worthwhile exercise, particularly if there are records that clearly help identify items of dissipation.

Reasonable Needs in the Future

Budgets or projections of future spending should be prepared, and the financial expert should take steps to verify the figures and determine if they are reasonable. What is reasonable? Of course, parties often disagree on what is reasonable. The financial expert should take an objective look at the standard of living during the marriage and then assess the future needs in light of that. Chapter 8 covers the development of budgets and projections in more detail.

What historical period should be evaluated when creating the budget? It is typical to evaluate one to five years of data, but there is no hard-and-fast rule for the time period that should be analyzed. Contrary to the position advanced in some divorces, future needs are not necessarily based only on expenditures in the last year of marriage. What if spending had been increasing by 10 percent per year for each of the last five years of the marriage? A case could be made that future needs should reflect a similar increase. What if spending was reduced prior to divorce because one spouse left a job to start a business? Should that lower spending be the basis for future needs, or should those future needs reflect the more "normal" historical spending?

The reasonable need of a spouse can become one of the most contentious areas of the standard of living analysis. What is really needed? Does a spouse need to continue to live the same lavish lifestyle as during the marriage? Or is need more narrowly defined to include a reasonable residence and associated living expenses? Was the lifestyle during the marriage needlessly frugal, and should the spouses be afforded a more expensive lifestyle based on the earnings of the parties?

One side may argue that the luxuries are not something a spouse is entitled to have paid for by the other spouse. The other side might well argue that even though the luxuries may not constitute "needs" as defined by the average person, those were part of the marital lifestyle and, therefore, should be part of the post-divorce lifestyle, regardless of who pays for it.

Whether or not a spouse will have partial or full custody of children may affect the calculation of reasonable needs as well. For example, if the spouse will not have overnight visits with the children, a smaller residence may be appropriate. In this case, the standard of living may need to be adjusted to account for a residence of smaller proportion but comparable quality to the marital residence.

Savings may also become an issue when evaluating the standard of living. Should a spouse's future needs only include living expenses, or should the spouse also be allocated funds for savings? This question becomes especially important when considering retirement savings. Suppose a married couple has been spending $3,500 per month on living expenses while saving $30,000 per year in the husband's retirement account. Following the divorce, the husband will continue to work and will continue to put money into the retirement account. If the wife does not work, she may not have an opportunity to save funds for her later years unless her spousal support includes money for this.

Admission of Evidence

As mentioned several times throughout this book, local laws will heavily influence the factors that will be considered relative to the standard of living. However, family law judges often have latitude in how they apply those laws, particularly in divorces that have unique circumstances not specifically addressed in the text of the laws. Cases involving clients with high net worth and/or very high earnings often have circumstances that fall outside the norm. Cases involving businesses or investments with uncommon facts will necessitate that the judge make a ruling that is not specifically addressed by the laws. In these cases, it may be possible to introduce concepts discussed in this chapter if they significantly impact the calculations.

Thus, the totality of the financial circumstances must be considered, and important relevant factors should be identified in each case. Local rules and case law should be evaluated to determine what evidence is likely to be admitted. Family courts often have latitude in considering and admitting evidence. Therefore, a strategy for persuading the court to admit evidence regarding other factors the forensic accountant believes are appropriate to include in the analysis of standard of living should be developed jointly between counsel and the expert.

Chapter 3

Defining and Calculating Income

Many different definitions of income can be used in family law cases. Local law will play a big part in defining income, but in more complicated cases, other definitions may come into play. The financial expert can help the attorneys and the court understand the various types of income and why they should be included or excluded from income calculations in a family law case.

Internal Revenue Service Definitions

The Internal Revenue Code is often a starting point for defining and quantifying income in family law cases. Experienced family lawyers know this is only the tip of the iceberg and does not cover many of the unusual situations arising in cases with complicated financial scenarios. However, because the Internal Revenue Service definition of income is so heavily relied upon in many divorces and child support cases, it must be addressed.

Following are items found on a personal federal income tax return. For more information on what these items of income can tell us about an individual's income or assets, refer to the more detailed discussion in Chapter 6.

The format of income tax returns changed slightly with the Tax Cuts and Jobs Act of 2017. A sample of a 2017 personal income tax return (Form 1040) is included in Appendix A to illustrate the format prior to the tax law change. A sample of the 2018 form is also included to show the new format. Form 1040 is much shorter in 2018; the new Schedule 1 was introduced to capture all the other sources of income that were removed from Form 1040. You may notice the line numbers on the new Schedule 1 correlate to the line numbers on the old Form 1040, presumably to reduce confusion.

Items of income on a personal income tax return are defined briefly here. Later in the book we will discuss how they are analyzed in the context of divorce and a lifestyle analysis. Items on Form 1040 include:

- Wages—This item includes compensation such as wages, salaries, tips, commissions, bonuses, fringe benefits, and other earnings reported to an employee on a W-2. The figure shown here is typically gross wages less deductible contributions to a retirement plan like a 401(k). Double check this to determine the true gross wages. If there have been deductible contributions to a retirement plan, the gross wages would be the wages on the income tax return plus the contributions.
- Interest—Both taxable and tax-exempt interest are reported on an income tax return, although only one type will be taxed. Both types of interest should be included in calculations regarding income, regardless of the taxability. Be sure, however, that the distinction between taxable and tax-exempt is noted when attempting to estimate income taxes to be paid in the future.
- Dividends—Stock dividends received via brokerage accounts or directly from individual investments will be reported here. The income tax return will note "qualified dividends," which is a portion of the total dividends receiving more favorable tax treatment. The figure that matters for income calculations in divorce is the total dividends received.
- IRAs, pensions, annuities—This item includes both early distributions and normal distributions after retirement. Both taxable and nontaxable distributions will be reported, and both are important for the income calculations related to divorce. If there was a lump-sum distribution, it should be determined how the funds were used or where the funds currently are.
- Social Security benefits—The total Social Security benefits and the taxable portion are reported on this line.

Items on Schedule 1 include:

- Taxable refunds or credits for state and local income taxes—This item might provide useful information during the lifestyle analysis but is typically not included in a calculation of income for support purposes. It may factor into an analysis of before-tax and after-tax income.
- Alimony received—This item will likely not be a factor in a current divorce. Under the new tax law, alimony is neither taxable to the recipient nor deductible by the payer. However, if a spouse was party to a divorce finalized before 2019, there may be alimony reported here.
- Business income or loss—Net income from a sole proprietorship or single member limited liability company (LLC) is reported here, with more details about income and expenses on Schedule C.
- Capital gain or loss—Gains from the sale of stock or other investment property are included here, with the details on Schedule D.
- Other gains or losses—This item includes the sale of property in a business, with the details reported on Form 4797. Since a sale of business property involves the disposition of assets, it may not be clear whether it is relevant to income calculations. However, it may be very relevant if the asset was depreciated in the past, thereby reducing historical income.
- Rental real estate, royalties, partnerships, S corporations, trusts—Net income from rental real estate or royalties is reported here, with the details of income and expenses on Schedule E, page 1. An owner's share of income from business ventures established as partnerships or S corporations is reported here, along with income from trusts. Additional details about the income are reported on Schedule E, page 2.
- Farm income or loss—Net income from farming activities is reported here, with the details of income and expenses reported on Schedule F.
- Unemployment compensation—Taxable unemployment compensation is reported here.
- Other income—A variety of items could be reported here, with some of the more common ones including gambling winnings, prizes and awards, and jury duty pay.

Nontaxable Income

An individual may receive many different types of income that are non-taxable for federal income tax purposes. It is important that these are not overlooked when doing a lifestyle because even though they are not taxed, they still represent income to the individual. Some of the more common types of nontaxable income include:

- Life insurance proceeds
- Disability benefits—Note that some disability benefits are taxable, while others are nontaxable.
- Child support
- Gifts and bequests—Many times gifts and inheritances are excluded from income for purposes of calculating support. However, these items should not be ignored altogether. It is still important to quantify them in case they might be relevant.
- Tax-exempt interest income
- Distributions from retirement accounts—For example, a distribution from a Roth IRA is generally not taxable, but there may be significant earnings on the contributions to the account. A Roth IRA may very well be part of an asset distribution in a divorce, but the impact of distributions on cash flow should also be considered.
- Compensation for injury or sickness
- Discharge of indebtedness—Sometimes debt forgiveness is a taxable item, whereas at other times it is nontaxable. This item is often overlooked in divorce proceedings, but it can be very important. Even though a spouse may claim that it is not real income, the spouse did receive money or value at some point in exchange for a promise to pay in the future. If the obligation to pay that debt is relieved, the money or property the spouse originally received should probably be considered income.
- Scholarships
- Meals and lodging provided by an employer, along with other perks like a company-owned vehicle used for personal purposes

- Gain on the sale of a principal residence
- Insurance reimbursements for living expenses
- Employer-provided education assistance
- Employer-provided dependent care assistance or child care benefits
- Moving expense reimbursement
- Foster care payments
- Other employer-provided fringe benefits
- Interest on savings for higher education

Reduction of Living Expenses

Some jurisdictions recognize that certain benefits or perks of employment or other business arrangements may not be considered income in the traditional sense, even though they may effectively reduce an individual's living expenses. Because these perks or benefits reduce the living expenses that must be paid out of pocket, they may be considered income for support calculations. Examples of such items include rent-free housing, meal allowances, memberships, or use of a company car for personal purposes.

Statutes Defining Income

State law and local laws often define what is included in income for family law cases. Even though each state's laws vary, the most common income items included are:

- Salaries, wages, and tips
- Commissions
- Bonuses
- Dividends
- Interest income
- Royalties
- Income from a trust or annuity

- Workers' compensation benefits
- Unemployment insurance benefits
- Disability insurance benefits
- Pensions
- Social Security benefits
- Alimony from an unrelated case
- Business income less business expenses
- Net rental income
- Stock options
- Severance pay

It does not matter if the item of income is taxable or nontaxable when calculating income for the purposes of divorce and support calculations. All that matters is whether the item falls under the definition of income, either because it is specifically defined or because it falls under a broad category of income.

Wisconsin law defines income in DCF 150 Child Support Percentage of Income Standard, the statute written by the Department of Children and Families and approved by the Wisconsin legislature. This language is provided as an example of a particularly comprehensive statute.

From DCF 150.02, income-related items are defined:

(13) "Gross income."
    (a) "Gross income" means all of the following:
        1. Salary and wages.
        2. Interest and investment income.
        3. Social Security disability and old-age insurance benefits under 42 USC 401 to 433.
        4. Net proceeds resulting from worker's compensation or other personal injury awards intended to replace income.
        5. Unemployment insurance.
        6. Income continuation benefits.
        7. Voluntary deferred compensation, employee contributions to any employee benefit plan or profit-sharing,

and employee contributions to any pension or retirement account whether or not the account provides for tax deferral or avoidance.

8. Military allowances and veterans disability compensation benefits.

9. Undistributed income of a corporation, including a closely-held corporation, or any partnership, including a limited or limited liability partnership, in which the parent has an ownership interest sufficient to individually exercise control or to access the earnings of the business, unless the income included is an asset under s. DCF 150.03 (4). In this paragraph:

    a. "Undistributed income" means federal taxable income of the closely held corporation, partnership, or other entity plus depreciation claimed on the entity's federal income tax return less a reasonable allowance for economic depreciation.

    b. A "reasonable allowance for economic depreciation" means the amount of depreciation on assets computed using the straight line method and useful lives as determined under federal income tax laws and regulations.

(14) "Income imputed based on earning capacity" means the amount of income that exceeds the parent's actual income and represents the parent's ability to earn, based on the parent's education, training and recent work experience, earnings during previous periods, current physical and mental health, history of child care responsibilities as the parent with primary physical placement, and the availability of work in or near the parent's community.

(15) "Income imputed from assets" means the amount of income ascribed to assets that are unproductive and to which income has been diverted to avoid paying child support or from which income is necessary to maintain the child or children at the standard of living they would have if they were living with both parents, and that exceeds the actual income from the assets.

(16) "Income modified for business expenses" means the amount of income after adding wages paid to dependent household members, adding undistributed income that the court determines is not reasonably necessary for the growth of the business, and subtracting business expenses that the court determines are reasonably necessary for the production of that income or operation of the business and that may differ from the determination of allowable business expenses for tax purposes.

Additional Wisconsin guidance is included in DCF 150.03, Support Orders:

(2) Determining income modified for business expenses. In determining a parent's monthly income available for child support under sub. (1), the court may adjust a parent's gross income as follows:
  (a) Adding wages paid to dependent household members.
  (b) Adding undistributed income that meets the criteria in s. DCF 150.02 (13) (a) 9 and that the court determines is not reasonably necessary for the growth of the business. The parent shall have the burden of proof to show that any undistributed income is reasonably necessary for the growth of the business.
  (c) Reducing gross income by the business expenses that the court determines are reasonably necessary for the production of that income or operation of the business and that may differ from the determination of allowable business expenses for tax purposes.
(3) Determining income imputed based on earning capacity. In situations where the income of a parent is less than the parent's earning capacity or is unknown, and in the absence of credible evidence to the contrary, the court may impute income to the parent at an amount that represents the parent's ability to earn, based on the parent's education, training and recent work experience, earnings during previous periods, current physical and mental health, history of child care responsibilities as the parent with primary physical placement, and the availability of work in or near the parent's community. If evidence is presented

that due diligence has been exercised to ascertain information on the parent's actual income or ability to earn and that information is unavailable, the court may impute to the parent the income that a person would earn by working 35 hours per week for the higher of the federal minimum hourly wage under 29 USC 206 (a) (1) or the state minimum wage in s. DWD 272.03. As an alternative to imputed income, the court may order the parent who is not a custodial parent to search for a job or participate in a work experience and job training program, including the Children First program under s. 49.36, Stats. If a parent has gross income or income modified for business expenses below his or her earning capacity, the income imputed based on earning capacity shall be the difference between the parent's earning capacity and the parent's gross income or income modified for business expenses.

(4) Determining income imputed from assets.

(a) The court may impute a reasonable earning potential to a parent's assets if the court finds both of the following:

1. The parent has ownership and control over any real or personal property, including but not limited to, life insurance, cash and deposit accounts, stocks and bonds, business interests, net proceeds resulting from worker's compensation or other personal injury awards not intended to replace income, and cash and corporate income in a corporation in which the parent has an ownership interest sufficient to individually exercise control and the cash or corporate income is not included as gross income under s. DCF 150.02 (13).

2. The parent's assets are underproductive and at least one of the following applies:

a. The parent has diverted income into assets to avoid paying child support.

b. Income from the parent's assets is necessary to maintain the child or children at the standard of living they would have had if they were living with both parents.

(b) The court shall impute income to assets by multiplying the
total net value of the assets by the current 6-month treasury bill
rate or any other rate that the court determines is reasonable and
subtracting the actual income from the assets that was included
as gross income under s. DCF 150.02 (13).

The vast majority of situations in Wisconsin will easily fall under these
laws, and the calculation of income will be clear. However, cases involving
business interests, real estate, income from investments, income from trusts,
and the like will be much more confusing.

Again, state statutes and case law will dictate the most relevant financial information in any case, but the guidance provided here is an example
of a fairly detailed set of laws. In contrast, the Uniform Interstate Family
Support Act provides only brief and general guidance on income for support purposes, stating:

"Income" includes earnings or other periodic entitlements to money
from any source and any other property subject to withholding for
support under the law of this state.

What Is Not Income?

There are a number of instances in which the receipt of funds will typically
not be considered income for support purposes. They include:

- Benefits paid under public assistance programs
- Student loans used for books and tuition
- Principal of life insurance death benefits (although interest or income
  on the benefits may be considered income)
- Stock that cannot be liquidated
- Return of principal or capital
- Stock received in connection with the sale of a business
- Equity in a principal residence

- Personal injury proceeds
- Nonmonetary gifts
- Future income that is considered speculative

Historical Earnings Analysis

Income can easily be determined in cases in which the party or parties only receive traditional wages. The rate of pay is constant, and it is easy to confirm historical earnings. The financial analyst must be careful to account for things like raises, overtime earnings, or periods during which a party does not work. However, as a general rule, past earnings can be easily analyzed, and future earnings are fairly predictable.

It is more difficult to analyze income when historical earnings fluctuate. This might happen because the earnings include things like bonuses, commissions, stock options, other incentive pay, or profit sharing. Remember, too, that earnings can go beyond what is reported on an income tax return. What is shown on an income tax return may not reflect the actual income or cash available to the spouse.

For example, commissioned salespeople can see wild fluctuations in their earnings based on changes in the economy, the industry, or the companies in which they work. A landscaping business will likely see income vary substantially throughout the year. Real estate developers may have modest income in some years but substantial income in other years, depending on the progress of projects. Corporate executives can see variations in their income related to bonuses and other incentive pay, which are often tied to the earnings of the company.

Some primary factors affecting the earnings of a traditionally employed individual include:

- Seasonality
- Promotions or demotions
- Other changes in job duties
- Changes in compensation structure

- Changes in the employer's business
- Changes in the industry
- Changes in general economic conditions

A self-employed individual can experience changes in income related to:

- Seasonality
- Expansion or contraction of the business
- Changes in the industry
- Changes in general economic conditions

Historical earnings will be evaluated using primarily income tax returns, wage statements, and pay stubs. However, as will be discussed in later chapters, earnings situations that go beyond traditional employment will require the analysis of other documents.

When analyzing historical earnings, the important procedures may include:

- Evaluating earnings over a period of one to ten years, paying attention to the total earnings and individual categories of earnings
- Looking for a trend in earnings between years
- Determining the reasons for any substantial changes in compensation
- Analyzing changes in earnings based on changes in rates of compensation, hours worked, and employers
- Evaluating how major changes in jobs and responsibilities have impacted annual earnings
- Comparing income tax returns and other documents to declarations, affidavits, or other representations made in the family law case

The historical earnings of the spouses is only one component of the financial analysis used to determine income for the purpose of calculating support.

Adjustments to Income

Some local laws specify adjustments that may be made when calculating income available for support, whereas other localities generally allow adjustments but do not specify the adjustments. Common adjustments to income related to business entities include things like depreciation, prepaid expenses, investment necessary to sustain or grow the business, or items of extraordinary income and expense. This list is not all-inclusive, as there can be many unusual situations that would be appropriate for an adjustment.

Cash Flow Versus Income

In some situations, income reported on a personal or business income tax return does not reflect the funds available to pay the family's living expenses. An example of the type of business venture that may exhibit this problem is real estate. Income tax laws related to real estate businesses are generally advantageous to the owners. That is, the level of deductions allowed to be taken for real estate ventures often results in little or no taxable income. However, the owners often find that the real estate venture provides ample cash flow, even in the absence of taxable income.

A different example would be a business venture that shows income on a tax return, with the spouse alleging that the income should not be included in support calculations because no cash was distributed to him or her. Often the contention is that the funds were "reinvested in the business" and therefore not available to pay support.

In the cash flow analysis, the forensic accountant will likely include items such as wages, interest, dividends, and cash distributions from business entities. The tax profit or loss from the business entities will be excluded from this analysis because the focus is the cash received. Items such as company fringe benefits and perks will likely be included in the cash flow analysis. Capital gains and losses may or may not be included in a cash flow analysis, depending on the circumstances of the case and the activities from which the capital gains and losses were realized.

Unfortunately, the cash flow versus income discussion is an area of great debate in family law cases. One side will inevitably argue that the earnings per the income tax return are very low, and therefore a very low level of support should be paid. The other side will argue that the earnings on the income tax return do not reflect the true income or cash flow of the spouse, so the cash flow should be the basis for support.

In the case of the spouse investing a business's earnings into growing the business or starting a new one, the argument may be that there is no cash flow available to pay support. The wording from the Wisconsin statute earlier in this chapter may be helpful to address this issue:

> "Income imputed from assets" means the amount of income ascribed to assets that are unproductive and to which income has been diverted to avoid paying child support or from which income is necessary to maintain the child or children at the standard of living they would have if they were living with both parents, and that exceeds the actual income from the assets.

The "investment" into a business may be considered an "unproductive asset" if that business is not generating income for the spouse. The investment in this unproductive asset can then lead to imputing income. This may be one way to address whether the spouse should be allowed to invest funds in the business and avoid having those funds included in income for purposes of support calculations.

As this is a gray area in family law, it is often difficult to predict how the court will interpret the financial facts. The financial expert should provide the court with multiple methods of calculating income. Ideally, each of the various methods will tend to support the results of the other methods of calculating income. Presenting the court with multiple methods of calculating income, all with results in a fairly narrow range, is more persuasive then presenting only one method of calculating income.

Earning Capacity and Imputed Income

In some cases, one or both parties may allege the other is not working at full earning capacity. This can happen when a person is unwilling or unable to work in his or her field of expertise or when he or she starts a new business, rather than earning wages through traditional employment. This may also happen if a party works less than full-time or only seasonally, or if the person chooses early retirement.

Caring for children at home may also impact a party's earning capacity, as it may prevent him or her from working full-time. A spouse or parent who has stayed at home for a period of time may have an earning capacity that could improve with education, training, and time in the workforce. Therefore, evaluation of an individual's earning capacity must be both short term and long term.

A spouse or parent leaving a job to start a business may also give rise to imputed income. A new business venture often has little to no income for a period of time that can span a number of years. It would seem unfair to the support recipient that the other party could leave a job with a stable income to start a business and avoid paying support because the new venture has no earnings. When a party has support obligations related to children or a former spouse, he or she is not necessarily entitled to start a business if that action results in reduced income. Imputing income could be very important in such situations.

If a party is not working or is working below his or her capacity, income may be imputed to that party in the family law case. A number of different factors may influence the imputed income, possibly including education, experience, economic conditions, and the local job market. In some cases, research on the job market and prevailing salaries will be sufficient. In other cases, a more detailed analysis is needed, possibly with the help of a vocational consultant who can evaluate an individual's skills, education, vocational opportunities, and earning capacity.

Chapter 4

Preparing for the Lifestyle Analysis

How can a family law attorney determine whether a lifestyle analysis is needed in a divorce case? A suspicious spouse may be all that is needed to begin a lifestyle analysis; however, a more objective basis for undertaking the lifestyle analysis is preferred. A lifestyle analysis can be expensive and time consuming, so doing a thorough evaluation of whether it is warranted and/or worthwhile under a cost/benefit scenario is a good idea. This chapter discusses numerous red flags that may indicate hidden income, hidden assets, or other financial irregularities, which are the types of things that could trigger the need for a lifestyle analysis.

Gathering documents early is a key part of the lifestyle analysis. By doing so, the attorney reduces the risk that documents will be altered or destroyed or that financial institutions will be unable to locate the documents. Although it can be a huge task to gather documents for all bank, brokerage, and credit card accounts, in addition to income tax returns and business documents, it is a critical component of the family law case.

Gathering documents should not be left until the last minute, as discovery deadlines can approach quickly. Attempting a lifestyle analysis at the last minute is risky and expensive. Extreme time limitations could impact how thorough and accurate the analysis is. A lifestyle analysis may uncover previously undisclosed accounts or assets, possibly creating a need for additional discovery, and tight litigation deadlines may cause a problem. If the attorney waits too long to retain an expert, it may not even be possible to find a forensic accountant who can meet the deadlines.

The lifestyle expert may need more than just documents. The divorcing spouses usually have important background information and details about financial transactions that can be invaluable to the lifestyle analysis. Unfortunately, the expert typically has access to only the spouse who retained his or her services. It is unusual that the spouse on the opposite side of the case is willing to sit down for an interview with the expert. However, it may be possible to obtain information from the other side through the discovery process by requesting additional documents, serving interrogatories, or deposing people with relevant information.

In this chapter, we will first discuss how the client can manage the financial aspects of divorce. Next we will cover the red flags of fraud in divorce. Finally, we discuss sources of information, strategies for gathering and managing documents, and the discovery process from the perspective of the financial expert.

Managing Financial Aspects of Divorce

When divorce is on the horizon, some clients do not know what to do about the financial aspect of the separation and divorce. The spouse who is in the lesser financial position (by virtue of either not being the major breadwinner or not having information about or control over the family finances) may not know where to begin.

The divorce attorney can provide the client with these simple (but sometimes overlooked) tips to assist in aggressively fighting the financial case in divorce court:

1. **Secure funds for living expenses, attorneys, and other professionals.** A spouse who does not control the family's finances may find it difficult to access funds during the divorce. It is not uncommon for the spouse in control of the finances to cut off access to money to force a quick (and possibly unfair) divorce settlement. Legal access to money is important, and the spouse must secure funds that will only be available to him or her. Relying solely on family court to award funding for living expenses and divorce professionals is far too risky.

(Sometimes the only option is to have the court order the disbursement of funds, but if the spouse has legal access to funds instead, securing those funds is advisable.)

2. **Any financial documents in the residence should be copied and put in a secure place outside the home.** The documents include income tax returns, bank and brokerage account statements, credit card statements, real estate closing statements, loan applications and contracts, documents related to major purchases, wills and trusts, and anything else related to the family's finances. If the client has legal access to account documents online, he or she should access and print all of the statements and related items. These are valuable documents needed during the divorce and it is unwise to rely on family court and the discovery process to get the documents.

3. **Make lists of all known assets, liabilities, real estate holdings, and business interests.** To ensure that everything is accounted for in the divorce, the client should not rely on his or her memory going forward. Important facts can be forgotten easily. The sooner the client makes lists of these items (and adds to them as details come to mind), the better the information that can be used to fight for a fair share. When hidden assets are suspected, lists like these can be one of the best starting points to search for the assets.

4. **Open accounts in his or her name only.** The spouse should get new bank accounts and credit cards, preferably with banks or companies that do not maintain the couple's joint accounts. This ensures that the spouse has accounts that are not accessible to the spouse, not even inadvertently. It may be difficult to secure credit if the spouse does not have a source of income or a separate credit history, but it is important to attempt to get credit. Once the divorce is final, he or she will need separate accounts, so starting the process sooner can be beneficial and can help protect the spouse's finances.

5. **Monitor credit regularly.** The spouse should immediately access his or her credit report and determine if there are any accounts of which he or she was not aware. This could reveal secret credit cards or other accounts the spouse used to engage in concealed business ventures or questionable activities such as affairs. Credit reports should be accessed

routinely during the divorce process to ensure that all liabilities have been accounted for in the divorce. Note that a person is not legally able to obtain the credit report of his or her spouse.

6. **Get a secure mailing address.** Secure a mailing address the other spouse is unable to access. This will be important because account statements, correspondence from counsel, and other mail can be received without fear of interception. A post office box may be the best option as it is both secure and private.

7. **Change beneficiaries and decision-makers.** The will and living will (or healthcare power of attorney) should be changed so the soon-to-be ex-spouse does not have decision-making authority. Beneficiaries for retirement accounts, life insurance policies, and other financial accounts should be changed. Although the spouse may still have a right to a portion of these assets before the divorce is final, steps should be taken to secure assets as much as possible.

8. **Prepare for a long fight and an outcome that might seem unfair.** Divorce can be a lengthy process, and the client must be prepared (both financially and emotionally) for a long fight. He or she should not assume the assets and liabilities will be divided in half. State laws vary, and spouses are not necessarily entitled to a 50/50 split in the divorce. However, if the client has the financial wherewithal to resist a quick settlement, he or she may have a better chance at a fair division of the assets.

Red Flags of Fraud in Divorce

The vast majority of family law cases are settled without trials. However, a client should not enter into a voluntary settlement if there are significant concerns about the truth of the financial disclosures and indications that assets or income may be hidden. Once a divorce case is resolved with a voluntary settlement, it is very difficult to reopen the case, even if there is a strong suspicion of fraud during settlement negotiations.

The first step in determining whether a forensic accountant is needed to evaluate the finances of the parties is the identification of red flags of fraud.

A red flag is simply a warning sign or an unusual item or circumstance. Red flags can be divided into four different categories:

- Behavioral—actions of the parties that seem secretive or suspicious
- Documentation—unusual characteristics of paper or digital documentation and data
- Personal—attributes of the personal finances that raise questions or indicate potential improprieties
- Business—aspects of the finances of a business that indicate something unusual or improper

Attorneys often use their instinct to determine when a forensic accountant is needed in a family law case. If something regarding the parties' finances does not feel right, it probably should be investigated. A client is often suspicious of the spouse before they are separated. The spouse may even be known to manipulate the money.

Beyond using intuition to determine if something is wrong, there are plenty of warning signs that indicate the finances should be evaluated carefully. These red flags by themselves do not mean money has disappeared or the finances are being manipulated, but they are signs that an investigation is warranted. Because divorce is so adversarial, it is likely that one or both of the spouses will conceal or manipulate financial facts.

Behavioral Red Flags

Evaluate the behavior of the spouse, both at home and at work. Is there secrecy or extreme control surrounding financial matters? Some general behavioral red flags include:

- Exerting excessive control over financial matters, such as control of all bank information, statements, and online access
- Concealing details of transactions from the spouse
- Making large expenditures or asset purchases without the knowledge of the spouse
- Being secretive about financial or other matters
- A history of deception

- Being focused on "getting one over" on others
- Asking or coercing a spouse to sign unusual financial or legal documents, especially with pressure to sign quickly and/or without advice from professionals
- Using a post office box or other private address to receive mail (which cannot be accessed by the spouse)
- Flaunting one's power or control over the other spouse
- Engaging in unnecessarily complicated transactions

Documentation Red Flags

The process of producing financial documents in a family law matter is often contentious, particularly in cases with larger income and asset values. The documentation can be voluminous, so it can take a great amount of time and effort to comply with discovery requests. Some of the more common discovery issues that can constitute red flags include:

- Variations between the financial disclosure form and supporting documentation
- Incomplete and/or unsigned financial disclosures
- Deleted computerized financial files, particularly QuickBooks or Quicken files or detailed spreadsheets
- Altered or destroyed financial documentation
- Backdated or falsely dated documents
- Refusal to produce relevant financial documents
- Piecemeal production of financial documents, especially in a confusing or redundant manner
- Deliberate attempts to delay or derail the financial portion of discovery
- Intentional confusion of financial records and paper trails of money

Personal Financial Red Flags

More specifically, the following financial red flags can point to the concealment of assets or income in the months or years leading up to a divorce:

- High volume of cash transactions, possibly aimed at avoiding a paper trail of the money
- Failure to deposit full paycheck or other known sources of funds

- Stockpiles of cash or other valuable assets
- Purposeful commingling of personal and business finances to obscure the financial picture
- "Loans" to friends or family members to reduce cash in the marital estate
- Undisclosed accounts, particularly if the accounts have current activity and/or substantial balances
- Emergence of once-hidden valuable assets during the marriage—If a party discovered throughout the marriage that the spouse was hiding valuable assets, it is likely that there are additional assets the party does not know about.
- Dramatic decrease in investment values
- Inflated or fabricated debts
- Depletion of marital property while leaving separate property untouched
- Engaging in expensive bad habits such as drugs or gambling
- Disappearance of assets known to exist during the marriage with no paper trail left
- Alleged decrease in personal income but no corresponding decrease in spending

One commonly occurring financial red flag is the substantial withdrawal of cash from a bank account, often multiple times. The spouse may also get cash into his or her hands by not depositing a full paycheck, cashing an undisclosed personal check, or through withdrawals at ATMs. The cash could be used to fund nonmarital expenses (such as an affair or secret business venture), purchase hidden assets, or add funds to undisclosed accounts. Cash may also be used to purchase cashier's checks or money orders that are hidden until the divorce is finalized.

Business Financial Red Flags

When a business is owned and operated by one of the spouses, there is always a risk of financial manipulation. When the spouses have operated a business together, a divorce or child custody case may create a situation in which they can no longer work together. There are often suspicions that the spouse who remains in control of the business is manipulating the finances.

Clearly, an owner or officer of a company exercises a level of control over the company that may allow him or her to manipulate the finances to his or her benefit in the divorce. The "out spouse" does not have direct access to documents and information about the inner workings of the business, so it is easy for the other spouse to conceal financial facts. Diverting funds to deprive the other party of a share of them is also a real possibility.

The presence of some of the following red flags may indicate the need for a forensic analysis of the business finances:

- Income tax returns cannot be reconciled with underlying records— While there are often certain differences between financial statements and income tax returns due to nuances in tax laws, the figures should still reconcile fairly easily.
- Apparently unreported income—A number of signs may point to a business underreporting its income. Bank deposits in excess of reported revenue or a lifestyle that exceeds reported income are two signs. When a business is allegedly losing money but continues to operate, accumulates assets, or remains relatively debt free, suspicions arise.
- Alleged decrease in business revenues but no corresponding decrease in expenses—This will be discussed in greater detail in Chapter 12.
- Decrease in revenues and/or profitability—A sudden decrease in revenue that corresponds with the filing of divorce is a common red flag. Does the decrease have a legitimate explanation? Does it pass the "smell test"? This is discussed in more detail in Chapter 12.
- Manipulation of business assets—Not recording valuable assets such as land, equipment, buildings, or intangible assets (goodwill, patents, etc.) could cause the overall value of the company to be depressed. The same is true for improperly valuing accounts receivable or inventory. Unusual fluctuations in the value of assets, particularly around the time of divorce, may be a red flag.
- Increase in expenses—A sudden increase in business expenses can be a red flag, especially when the change occurs around the time the family law case is initiated. One of the potential schemes is creating and paying phony vendors to inflate expenses and therefore reduce the profits of the company. At the same time that the profits are artificially depressed, cash is also diverted from the company.

- Increase in liabilities—Higher debts translate into a less valuable business. The debts could be phony, recorded simply to manipulate the value of the company. The debts could be legitimate but incurred simply to encumber the asset to manipulate the property division in the divorce.
- Transfers of funds to and from the owner—While small businesses often receive cash infusions from their owners, the loaning of money to the business (or the owner borrowing money from the business) can be suspect. These types of transactions can easily be used to hide money or otherwise obscure financial details.
- Personal expenses paid by the business—Business owners and executives often use business funds to pay personal expenses but record them as business expenses in the accounting records. This decreases the company's profits. It also means the owner or executive does not need as large a paycheck, as there are fewer personal expenses to pay with personal funds. The reduced profits and smaller paycheck can have a significant impact on both property division and support calculations.
- Related party transactions with family members, friends, or close business associates—These are particularly suspicious if the business has never before transacted with these related parties. They may be sham transactions or detrimental to the business so as to reduce the value or profitability of the business.
- Commingling funds between multiple business interests—Moving funds haphazardly between business ventures or commingling the finances of multiple business ventures may be designed to confuse the finances and make sorting out the money between entities impossible.
- Creation of new entities to divert assets—A spouse may establish a new entity simply as a vehicle to divert cash and other valuable assets. Entities formed in the period leading up to separation should be critically evaluated to determine whether there are legitimate business activities or whether transactions are shams to deprive the spouse of a share of assets.
- Elimination of owner's paycheck—It is not unusual for the owner of a closely held business to reduce or eliminate his or her paycheck around the time of divorce. This may be done in an attempt to make it appear there is no income available for support. Even a nonowner employee could have a paycheck temporarily reduced or eliminated, with an

agreement that the employee will receive all the back pay after the divorce is finalized.

- Transfer of ownership or control—If an owner or executive of a closely held business gives up ownership or control of the company around the time of separation, the transfer of ownership or control could be a sham. It might also be legitimate but done to manipulate the finances and operations of the business.

If the forensic accountant questions the authenticity or accuracy of business financial data and documents, he or she can turn to alternative sources of information against which to compare the suspect information. For example, if a self-employed dentist is suspected of underreporting his income after separation to manipulate support calculations, the accountant should look at other sources of information that could indicate whether income has been properly reported.

Appointment books might provide information about the level of activity in the practice. The number of appointments held over a period of several years may demonstrate that there has not been a decline in activity. Consistency in appointments between pre-separation and post-separation periods would tend to indicate that the dentist's income has not decreased.

The level of expenses in the dental practice may also provide clues to the level of activity and, therefore, the expected level of income. Certain expenses tend to move in conjunction with the level of activity. For example, lab expenses often move up or down in the same way that revenue increases or decreases. If the dentist claims a drop in income but lab expenses have not decreased accordingly, this may be a sign that the dentist is deliberately underreporting income in the practice. In service businesses such as a dental practice, the level of payroll expenses is often a good indicator of the volume of business being done. Employees are needed in proportion to the number of patients being seen and procedures being done, and an analysis of wages versus revenues over time may provide insight into claims about a dental practice's income.

The business lifestyle analysis will be discussed in great detail in Chapter 12. The information there focuses on common areas of abuse within the financial statements and accounting records, the way problems are identified, and the techniques used to determine the truth behind the reported numbers. Brief case studies are provided as examples of the types of findings that may result from the business lifestyle analysis.

The Next Step

Identifying red flags during the divorce process does not automatically mean that the client must spend thousands of dollars on a full forensic workup. In fact, many times it is preferable to take the process slowly and perform the work in phases. A good forensic accountant will help the client spend money in the most strategic way possible.

Initially, it may be enough to have a financial expert look at the financial disclosure forms, income tax returns, and other selected financial documents to get a feel for the situation. The expert might immediately see things that do not make sense and warrant further investigation. Alternatively, the forensic accountant may see that everything looks to be in order and may determine that further analysis probably would not yield any useful results.

In either case, the initial workup of the numbers can be done with a limited budget. The client can then decide if it makes sense to expand the scope of work to encompass more of the detailed documents. In larger cases, there may even be five or six phases to the work. As each step ends, the attorney, the client, and the forensic accountant can decide whether it is beneficial to the case to proceed with the next step.

The lifestyle analysis is not an inexpensive undertaking. Certainly, basic procedures can be done with a limited budget. A simplistic analysis of transactions can also be done with limited funds. But if a detailed analysis of banking and credit card transactions is needed for a period of three years or more, the client should know it could cost at least several thousand dollars. Complex cases can easily reach tens of thousands of dollars.

The decision to proceed with a forensic analysis of the finances is all about the cost versus benefits. How likely are we to find financial improprieties? What is the estimated value of the concealed assets or income? How much could the spouse reasonably expect to recover in court? What will be the cost of the analysis?

In one case, a husband and wife had ownership interests in eight different companies, all in the hospitality field. One company was larger and the other seven were smaller companies for special projects. The married couple had made a lot of money throughout the years, and the division of assets was proceeding amicably. However, the wife had concerns that the husband may have concealed assets, particularly since funds had been transferred back and forth between the various companies.

The wife asked for an analysis of the funds distributed from each of the companies to the husband to determine whether those funds were deposited into the family's personal accounts. It was a $10,000 investment in services. As a result of an analysis of the income tax returns, accounting records of the companies, and personal bank accounts, it was found that $150,000 in expense reimbursements issued to the husband was never deposited into family bank accounts. If we assume that the wife is entitled to half of that value, her $75,000 share of the assets was well worth the cost of the investigation.

Of course, the wife did not know at the outset what would be found. However, there was enough suspicion and enough money at stake overall to believe that the funds would be well spent. The client believed that even if nothing was found, the investment of $10,000 was worth the peace of mind she would have from knowing she did her due diligence.

Financial Disclosures

The financial disclosures made in a family law case are critical pieces of information. Early on, spouses may be careless with their disclosures, assuming that they can be more precise or thorough later in the case. Such an approach is ill-advised, as inaccurate or untruthful disclosures can impact the credibility of the spouse throughout the case.

Financial disclosures are often made well in advance of retaining an expert to perform a lifestyle analysis. However, starting the lifestyle analysis early can be of great benefit to counsel and the client. A lifestyle analysis can help ensure that disclosures are as accurate as possible. More importantly, the lifestyle analysis has the potential to be the roadmap for the rest of discovery. As the forensic accountant uncovers interesting financial details, additional subpoenas can be issued, more assets can be uncovered, and more sources of income can be identified and thoroughly investigated.

Financial Affidavits

During the divorce process, both spouses are required to disclose certain financial information. This may take the form of responses to interrogatories, financial affidavits, or other similarly titled declarations. These representations about the financial details are important because they provide a starting point for analyzing income and assets, as well as searching for hidden assets. In addition, if false disclosures (or failures to disclose) are made at this stage of the divorce process, the credibility of the spouse may be damaged for the duration of the case.

The financial expert can help prepare the financial affidavits to increase their accuracy and reliability. Even if the expert has not prepared the financial affidavit, he or she should still examine it carefully as part of the forensic accounting process in the divorce case.

Marital Balance Sheet

If marital balance sheets were prepared prior to the retention of the financial expert, the expert should examine them. If a balance sheet has not been prepared, the expert will likely create one in the early stages of work. The marital balance sheet is an important piece of the puzzle for any financial expert, and multiple balance sheets may be created to document the changes in assets and liabilities over time.

The marital balance sheet should include the following information and classifications:

- Assets and liabilities listed using their formal name and last four digits of account numbers, if applicable (include both open and closed accounts for completeness)
- Common names for the asset and liability accounts, if the parties used names other than the formal names
- Balances or valuations
- Dates of balances (from statements or valuations)

- Notations regarding the documentation in support of the balances or valuations
- Comments or important notes related to the assets and liabilities
- Classification of assets and liabilities as separate or marital
- Proposed division of marital assets

Balances, valuations, classifications, and divisions may not be known immediately. Often, the marital balance sheet will be a working document that changes frequently while the forensic accountant is investigating.

Investigating People

The numbers in a divorce case cannot be investigated without knowing things about the people involved. This includes not only personal information, but also information about the people they know and the companies with which they are involved.

Background checks can provide a wealth of information on people and business interests and may uncover information that leads to the discovery of hidden assets or undisclosed streams of income. Simple Internet searches can turn up interesting information but often are not enough. If someone is actively concealing business interests or other assets, it is unlikely that information about those things will be readily available with a couple of searches.

In his book *The Art of Fact Investigation: Creative Thinking in the Age of Information Overload* (Ignaz Press 2016), attorney and investigator Philip Segal explains:

> The most important reason Google is never enough is that most of the critical documents you need are not on Google. Google has not scanned and indexed all public records in the United States. Most U.S. counties (and many places in the rest of the world) require that to see public records, a person has to go down to the relevant government office and either make paper copies of whatever he needs or look on that agency's own computers that are not connected to the Internet.

Even information you find online may not be sufficient. Suppose you see on a county website that a company you suspect of being linked to your opponent bought a building. To find out who signed the mortgage on behalf of that company, you will usually be required to get down to the county records office and view the document for yourself—or, more commonly, send a record retriever to do it for you.

Mr. Segal offers a test to determine how much information is available about someone online. Do a search on yourself and see how much is revealed about your personal history, finances, and relationships. He suggests about one percent of your information is available, with missing data including things like all of the people you have ever worked with, all of your contractual obligations, the limited liability companies you own, the complete record of the court cases in which you have been involved, and more.

Another overlooked fact about search engines is that they are not neutral sources of information. A search engine is a business, and as such, it has an incentive to prioritize certain search results over others. The search engine may deem one result to be of higher quality than another and present it far ahead of the other. Yet the result that is pushed down by the search engine may be important information that you need.

Mr. Segal further notes that search engines are not sufficient for background investigations because they cannot make complex connections between sets of facts like an investigator can. When a fact is found about a person or entity, there is often a next search that needs to be done. Discovery of a person in a particular profession may lead to the need for a professional license search, which may lead to the need for a search of disciplinary history, which could uncover a related party who should be vetted, and so on. A search engine by itself cannot take these next steps, and an investigator is necessary to evaluate the data and work through the process.

A professional investigator is necessary if a thorough background investigation is needed. The typical forensic accountant or other financial expert should not be relied on for this work. You need a private detective who is skilled at digging into people's backgrounds. In addition to finding important facts, the work of an investigator may be used to impugn the credibility of a witness or party to the divorce.

Sources of Private Records

Private records are the lifeblood of the financial portion of the family law case. It is therefore important to know the primary sources of records and why they are important. Roadblocks during discovery can be more easily removed if the attorney understands the importance of the documents, what they are commonly called, and where they are held.

Every transaction generates a paper trail with multiple pieces of paper (either digital or hard copy). Therefore, the forensic accountant may often look for more than one document or piece of evidence behind a transaction to determine its true nature. Documents created by third parties are generally more reliable than those created by the parties to the litigation. Third parties such as banks or credit card companies have no direct interest in the litigation and therefore have little reason to falsify or manipulate records, so their records are generally deemed authentic and accurate.

Banks, Brokerages, and Credit Card Companies

Records held by banks, brokerages, and credit card companies may be some of the most important documents in a financial investigation for a family law case. These documents provide the details of sources and uses of funds, and they do not lie. They are often the key to finding hidden sources of income and hidden assets, as we will see in Chapters 9 and 10. In addition to subpoenaing documents related to known accounts, it is important to ensure that the document request includes general language that requires disclosure of all accounts and related documents.

Parties to a divorce sometimes do not know which banks to subpoena, particularly if there is a suspicion of hidden accounts. In this case, financial investigators look for clues to banking relationships. The most obvious place to look for bank names is the tax return, as it often includes line items for interest income or mortgage interest expense.

A search for real estate transaction recordings should be done, as mortgage companies will be identified through this process. A search for other credit facilities secured by real estate, inventory, or other assets should also be done. These will identify the lenders and may give clues to other assets that were previously undisclosed. An evaluation of bank statements, broker-age statements, and credit card statements for known accounts may reveal additional undisclosed accounts, as the statements may show transfers or other transactions involving other banks. A transaction involving a "new" bank may be a good reason to send a subpoena to that institution to see if the spouse has any accounts there.

When these avenues have been exhausted, the spouse and attorney may simply guess at which banks to subpoena. An educated guess at a favorite bank for a spouse may yield results. Worst case scenario, the guess is wrong and the bank responds that no records are available.

Lenders

Loan applications related to home mortgages, automobile loans or leases, personal loans, or commercial loans can provide a wealth of information. Assets, liabilities, and income sources must be disclosed on loan applica-tions, and sometimes supporting documentation is required. Individuals applying for loans may be motivated to make the financial picture look as positive as possible. The applicant may fully disclose all income sources and assets to the lender. If income sources and assets have not been fully disclosed in the divorce, the loan application may be used to impeach the spouse's credibility.

Loan applications can be acquired by sending subpoenas to banks and lending institutions. If the spouse attempts to quash the subpoena, this is a sign that there may be very interesting information in the loan documents. Courts are not always willing to use data on loan applications as evidence of assets to be divided in the divorce, especially if the applicant testifies that the application is not completely accurate. However, at the very least, that spouse can be shown to be dishonest and that could call into question other representations made during the family law case.

Taxing Authorities

The parties to a divorce or child support action often have copies of their income tax returns, and those should be produced during discovery. How-ever, sometimes the parties do not have copies of the tax returns or one party disputes the authenticity of the tax returns. In these cases, the income tax returns can be retrieved from the taxing authorities directly by filling out the proper forms and having the proper signatures.

Usually the parties will seek the federal income tax return, which is requested with Form 4506, Request for Copy of a Tax Return, but state tax returns may be sought as well. Note that Form 4506 can be used to request either personal or business tax returns. The fee is $50 per return, and returns up to six years old can be requested. Alternatively, Form 4506-T, Request for Transcript of Tax Return, can be used for free, but only for personal income tax returns going back as far as three years. The transcript will show most of the lines from the income tax return but will not give all of the details. It will provide the information as originally filed by the taxpayer but will not reflect any amended returns or adjustments made by the Internal Revenue Service.

Income tax returns are not the only tax documents that can be obtained from the government. Estates and trusts may file tax returns that have important information. Businesses may file several different types of tax forms with state or local governments, including sales tax returns, payroll tax returns, personal property tax returns, manufacturing property tax returns, fuel tax returns, and more. These documents can provide information that may be helpful when evaluating financial disclosures made during the family law case. It may not be immediately obvious what can be gleaned from those other types of tax returns, but in general, they may provide hints about levels of activity and seasonality of the business. Conflicting numbers between various tax returns may indicate areas needing further investigation.

Credit Reporting Agencies

It is important to obtain credit reports for both spouses during the divorce process. The credit reports ensure the parties are aware of all credit accounts in their names and may also help point to previously unknown assets or liabilities. Further, a review of credit reports will help the spouses identify any derogatory information that may limit opportunities to credit in the future.

Note that a spouse is entitled to access only his or her own credit report. The other spouse's credit report is off limits unless proper authorization is received. It may be tempting for one spouse to skirt the rules and access the credit report without authorization, but it is advised to avoid doing this as it may create credibility issues.

Accountants

It may be advisable to subpoena an accountant who has prepared tax returns or financial statements for the divorcing couple. It is sometimes easier to get the documents from the accountant than from the spouse. Ensure that the subpoena includes not only the income tax returns or financial statements that were prepared but also all supporting documentation, work papers, and any correspondence. Essentially, everything in the possession of the accountant should be subpoenaed in the interest of being thorough.

Employers

Employment records can be obtained directly from an employer with a subpoena. Why might these records be important? They will help confirm hours worked, rates of pay, gross pay, deductions, and more. Important information can be discovered about the spouse's work history and benefits (such as perks, stock options, bonuses, and retirement). When details of the family's finances are in question, employment records can be helpful to confirm the financial facts.

Other Private Records

Occasionally, the sources of documents discussed to this point are insufficient to fully untangle the financial web. The holders of the records may be uncooperative, or they simply may not have what is needed. This is when counsel and the financial expert need to get creative to find other sources of records that may provide clues about assets, earnings, and spending.

A few examples of alternative sources of data include telephone companies, shipping companies like United Parcel Service or FedEx, utilities, airlines, and automobile dealerships. Information from these sources can point to business relationships, business activity such as sales and shipments to customers, travel activity, and major expenditures.

Consider an analysis of a laundromat, which reported dramatically decreased revenues following the filing of the divorce action. Counsel subpoenaed records from the water company showing the amount of water used on a monthly basis for the last several years. The records showed that the water usage did not go down, calling into question the claims of declining revenues. This was a compelling argument, as it is easy to understand that if the water usage at a laundromat is consistent, then the level of revenues is likely also consistent.

Caution!

Be wary of private investigators who claim they can access private records for a fee. The techniques they use may not be legal and could damage the credibility of your case. They may be getting information using hackers or the "dark web," both of which involve illegality. It is also common to pretext (pretend to be someone else) to get information, which is unethical at best and illegal at worst. Accessing financial records and other private records using false pretenses and/or without proper authorization is usually unlawful. Even though obtaining information may be critical, it is ill-advised to risk damaging the credibility of the client and the case in the pursuit of this information.

Sources of Public Records

Public records can provide a tremendous amount of information for use in family law proceedings. The previously discussed private records are often the best sources of information used to find hidden assets when performing a lifestyle analysis; however, many other public records can also provide valuable information. The most common public records relate to real estate and mortgages. In addition, other publicly available information can help provide background data on a spouse and his or her business ventures. Key relationships can be uncovered in public records as well.

Real Estate Records

Real estate records, including property transfer, ownership, and tax records, are best used to help identify undisclosed assets. Property ownership records are found at the recorder's office (register of deeds), whereas property tax records are found at the assessor's office. These records will document ownership of the property (both past and present), legal descriptions, buildings on the property, sales price and date, assessed value of the property, tax bills, tax payments, and mortgages on the property. In addition, real estate records might provide clues about people and their relationships.

Court Records

Court records can provide information on people, companies, relationships, and financial matters. Names of individuals as well as the companies they are associated with should be searched for both civil and criminal records.

- Civil cases often include financial matters, so there may be information on the existence and value of assets and the profitability of business ventures in the court filings. The records often point to related parties such as relatives, friends, coworkers, or business associates. An investigation into these related parties may uncover previously unknown assets or business ventures.
- Criminal cases of a financial nature may provide information that can be used in a lifestyle analysis. Cases involving fraud or other white-collar crime may have useful financial information. In criminal cases of any type, there may be information about people or businesses with which the spouse is involved.
- Bankruptcy court records provide tremendous amounts of financial information. Both personal and business bankruptcy records should be searched for evidence of undisclosed assets, business interests, or other property of value.
- Probate court records can provide information on assets and related parties, which may point to previously undisclosed assets. These records may be helpful for uncovering business interests, investments, and other valuable assets that may have been inherited.

Note that many court records can be found online. Many state and local courts provide online access to records, with documents ranging from basic docket information to actual documents filed in cases. Courts that do not provide copies of documents filed in cases online often provide them via fax or mail with a proper request (and usually a nominal fee). U.S. federal courts provide filings online through PACER (Public Access to Electronic Court Records), which are available for relatively nominal fees. RECAP is an online service that collects federal court documents purchased by consumers through PACER and provides free access to those documents to the public.

Corporate Records

Corporate records are maintained by states and include registration of corporations, partnerships, and limited liability companies. Some state or local governments also require registration of individuals or entities doing business as (DBA) an entity that is not one of these three basic types. Corporate record keepers collect registration information including the name of the business, the registered agent, and the address. Most states do not track details like owners or members of boards of directors, although some may gather this information and make it available either on paper or online.

Uniform Commercial Code Records

Uniform Commercial Code (UCC) filings are made when businesses receive financing that is secured by business assets such as equipment, inventory, accounts receivable, furniture, or fixtures. A mortgage is filed for financing related to real estate, while a UCC filing is for financing linked to personal property. UCC filings can help identify assets owned by a company, find the lenders, and determine who might have rights to the company's assets. These filings are recorded with the county Register of Deeds or with the state UCC office, depending on the state in which the filing occurred and the type of collateral.

Tax Liens

Tax liens can be filed for unpaid real estate, sales, income, withholding, unemployment, or personal property taxes. Liens are filed against property owned by the taxpayer who owes the debt and are generally not released until the lien is satisfied.

Many tax records related to the liens are generally private, but the filing of a lien for unpaid taxes is usually public. The Internal Revenue Service maintains an Automated Lien System (ALS) Database Listing, which provides information on business tax liens. The information can be obtained by purchasing a quarterly listing from the U.S. Treasury or through a database service such as LexisNexis.

States have also taken to publishing databases of tax "deadbeats," citing individuals and businesses who have the largest unpaid tax bills. A tax lien may indicate the existence of previously unknown income or assets and may provide clues about the financial health of a business or person.

Databases

Several companies provide access to data aggregated from many different databases. The databases include information from credit-reporting agencies, public records, court records, and more. The databases can provide information on a person's current and former addresses, vehicle ownership, relatives and associates, real estate ownership, business affiliations, and more.

All databases are not alike. There are "free" options available on the Internet, although the free or low-cost searches often end up costing much more by the time you purchase the reports you need. Subscription-based services available to private investigators are often much more powerful.

Even though these databases provide a lot of information on people, the information is incomplete and is not always accurate. Information found through database searches should be checked against source documents if it is going to be used substantively in the divorce case. Also, note that the information is rarely complete, so it should not be the sole source of information about the spouses.

It is also important to note that access to these databases is often controlled because they include nonpublic personal information. Laws like the Gramm-Leach-Bliley Act (GLBA) restrict the use of this data, and therefore anyone accessing it needs to have a "permissible purpose." Examples of permissible purposes include fraud prevention or detection, legal compliance, or transactions authorized by the consumer.

Motor Vehicle Records

Motor vehicle records provide the name, address, vehicle identification number, and titleholder of a vehicle. These records are sometimes difficult to access, but it is often advisable to attempt to get them to help identify valuable assets.

Professional Licensing

States require licenses for a variety of professionals, including doctors, attorneys, private detectives, physical therapists, accountants, cosmetologists, and massage therapists. The licensing and credential data is generally available to the public and may include information about employers and disciplinary proceedings.

Public Company Information

The Securities and Exchange Commission maintains records in searchable databases that can help uncover significant ownership interest in public companies or determine the compensation of executives and board members. Buy and sell information for stockholders with more than a 10 percent interest is publicly available, as are stock ownership records for the officers and directors of public companies. Financial statements and other filings made with the Securities and Exchange Commission give information on salaries, bonuses, stock options, and other compensation of certain executives of public companies.

Intellectual Property

Information on copyrights, patents, and trademarks for which companies apply can be found at the U.S. Patent and Trademark Office. This information may be important in finding undisclosed business interests or intellectual property that may not be disclosed in the divorce. These items could have substantial value.

Business and Industry Databases

Hoovers and Dun & Bradstreet (D&B) are the oldest and best-known organizations that have amassed data on companies and the industries in which they operate. In recent years D&B acquired Hoovers and branded the new products as D&B Hoovers. The databases available through D&B Hoovers contain information on the owners, officers, executive compensation, company financial statements, key ratios, and creditors.

There are other providers of such information, but as the digital landscape changes quickly, so do the providers. The key is to find a reliable provider that is comprehensive in the sources of data from which it draws.

Internet and Search Engines

Search engines have made it easy to find information on people and companies. Effectively using search engines can result in valuable information about relationships between people, the existence of assets and business ventures, and the particulars about businesses. This information may be useful in a contentious divorce case. But it is important to remember that search engines will reveal only a small fraction of information available about people and businesses. There is so much more information to be known than an Internet search will ever find.

Effectively using search engines has become an art, with users making searches broader or narrower based on the number and quality of results returned to them. For example, suppose you are searching for information about a man with a fairly common last name. A search using just his name will yield too many results to be useful. The search should be narrowed using unique pieces of information known about the person. Those identifiers that help your search efforts may be an employer, a job title, a name of a friend or relative, a hobby, or anything that might help identify the correct man with the common last name. Based on information discovered with each search, additional searches can be crafted to dig further into available information.

Although it may take some time to find information pertaining to the spouse in question, the effort is often worthwhile, especially if the spouse is suspected of hiding assets, income, or business relationships and involvements. Internet searches do not take the place of a background investigation by a qualified private investigator, however. There are many sources of information on people and companies that cannot be accessed through a search engine, and it takes an experienced investigator to find many details. Consider the information found by an amateur with a search engine to be merely the beginning of what may be found about a person or organization.

Social Networking Sites

Social networking sites have created additional sources of information for family law cases. People create detailed profiles including friends, vital statistics, work and education history, and other private information. They may post status updates that include their whereabouts, relationships with others, and photographs of activities. Current popular social media sites include Facebook, Instagram, LinkedIn, Twitter, Snapchat, and dating sites like Match.com. New sites and apps are always popping up, so this list could change quickly.

Inferences might be drawn about personal relationships and business ventures, with clues about them often revealed on social networking sites. The expert is cautioned to use the information carefully and to attempt to validate and verify any information that may become important to the family law case. Counsel is cautioned against creating fake profiles on social media sites or otherwise attempting to gain access to others' accounts under false pretenses. Being dishonest to get information from a social media site may damage credibility or taint the information retrieved. In some instances, it may also be a violation of professional rules or laws.

Information from Clients

Often it is necessary to rely on clients for certain information in a family law case. The face of a bank statement or financial statement provides limited information, and sometimes the client needs to explain an expenditure or process. Without information from the client, it may be impossible to interpret the data or make calculations related to the lifestyle.

There are dangers in relying on information from clients. The client may be blatantly deceptive, and the attorney and financial expert may know it. Maybe the client falls into a gray area where he or she is known to stretch the truth. Possibly the client has always appeared trustworthy, but no one knows for sure if that impression is correct.

Miles Mason of Miles Mason Family Law Group provides the following guidance on evaluating information provided by the client to the forensic accountant:

What happens if a CPA fails to question facts provided by a client? Every CPA has duties imposed upon them by the Independence and Due Professional Care requirements of the AICPA's Code of Professional Conduct. Most experienced CPAs will admit that they have a duty to look critically at financial information obtained from a client. Even further, some experienced forensic accountants may say that, depending on the circumstances, they may even be required to discount potentially biased input from a client. Let's discuss two scenarios.

Scenario One. Tom is the supported spouse. In his monthly statement of income and expenses, Tom claims he spends $600 per month on groceries for himself and only $200 per month for the parties' two small children. The forensic accountant may not be required to confirm or question these estimates given the relative affluence of the couple and general lifestyle. Based on the professional judgment of the CPA, no additional confirmation may be required. Professional judgment results from the CPA's years of education, training, experience, and good old-fashioned common sense.

Scenario Two. On the same monthly income and expenses summary, Tom claims he spends $1,500 monthly on gas. This should call for more investigation. The CPA must take some additional steps to confirm the claimed amount. Additional steps should include asking Tom how he routinely pays for gas. If Tom's answer is with credit cards, determine which ones. Take a look at the monthly statements for those cards. Add up total gas charges over a relevant time period. The CPA cannot afford to blindly accept any number simply because the client says so. If the CPA does blindly accept the client's numbers, the CPA is just begging to be cross-examined on the lack of independence and failure to exercise due professional care.

Beginning the Engagement

A successful engagement with a forensic accountant in a family law case starts by setting the stage for the work to be performed. One of the most important steps is developing the scope of the engagement. There are almost always limitations on the work based on budgets, deadlines, and available documentation. Therefore, it is important to evaluate what is available, what work is most critical and will be most valuable, and what problems the limitations might cause.

The typical forensic accounting engagement will follow this general process:

1. Secure the engagement—Determine the nature of the engagement, the identities of the parties involved, and whether there are any conflicts of interest. Determine whether work can be completed in the time frame identified by the client, and whether the forensic accountant has the necessary expertise and resources to complete the engagement.

2. Define the scope of the engagement—Agree on what is to be accomplished by the financial expert. This includes identifying:
   • The issues on which to focus
   • The time period to cover
   • Documents that will be required
   • The level of detail that will be analyzed
   • Investigative techniques to be used
   • Which staff members will perform the work
   • What must be included in the final report
   • Deadlines for interim reports and the final report

   Often the complete scope of the work is not known up front. At times there are questions as to what documents will be obtained and how detailed they will be. In cases like this, the forensic accountant's work may take a phased approach, in which a small scope is contemplated initially, and additional work will be agreed to once more is known.

For example, it is not unusual for the financial expert to do an initial workup of the income tax returns and financial statements to determine whether there are any red flags of fraud or other irregularities. After that is completed, the expert is in a better position to make recommendations about additional work. The expert will often have a good feel for whether additional work will yield beneficial results. Since budgets are often a chief concern of clients, breaking the work down into pieces may be more beneficial than immediately agreeing to a large scope of work.

3. Determine fees and payment arrangements—Whether the engagement will be billed using hourly fees or a fixed fee, the fees and payment requirements should be outlined in the engagement letter. It may be preferable to address the engagement agreement to the attorney and have the attorney pay the fees. This will ensure that the expert's work is protected as work product, as discussed in Chapter 1. Alternatively, the engagement letter could be addressed to the client with the client paying the expert directly. The procedure depends on the preference of the family lawyer.

4. Conduct background work—In the early stages of the engagement, the forensic accountant gathers background information to assist with the financial analysis. This portion of the engagement will include:
   - Interviewing involved parties, although the expert usually will not have an opportunity to talk to the opposing party
   - Providing discovery assistance
   - Performing background research

5. Analyze data—The financial analysis is discussed in detail in Chapter 7.

6. Reporting—Chapter 13 covers the report, either oral or written, of the financial expert.

7. Testifying—Providing deposition and trial testimony is discussed in Chapter 13.

Chapter 5

Financial Discovery

Discovery for the financial portion of the family law case can be time-consuming, particularly for cases involving high-net-worth or high-income spouses. There may be many accounts with a high volume of transactions, creating thousands of pages of paper or digital financial documents. Unfortunately, this process is a necessary part of family law cases, particularly if there are multiple sources of income, if the totality of the family's assets is unknown, or if a number of the red flags discussed in Chapter 4 are present.

Even though documents can be obtained during discovery through informal requests for them, it is not advisable to rely on an informal process for gathering data. What happens if a key account is "forgotten" in the process? By making the demand for documents formal, a paper trail has been established, and the party can be held accountable for failing to disclose that account and the relevant documents.

Reliability of Records

Which financial records produced in the family law case should be considered reliable? One of the most important factors to consider is the source of the documents. The most reliable documents come from disinterested third parties. For example, parties such as banks, insurance companies, and title companies, which have no apparent interest in the family law case and no

apparent personal relationship with either of the spouses, tend to keep very reliable records. Since they have no personal interest in the divorce (and likely no knowledge of it), they have no motive for manipulating records or documents prior to producing them.

On the other hand, documents and records created and maintained by the spouses or people close to them are more likely to be manipulated. Check registers, asset listings, and other documents prepared by the parties to the family law case are subject to manipulation, and, therefore, the financial expert should think carefully before relying on such documents as a primary source of information for the lifestyle analysis.

Documents Needed for the Lifestyle Analysis

Appendix B has a comprehensive list of financial documents that may be requested and subpoenaed in family law cases. While no such list can cover every possible scenario, this list is likely comprehensive for the vast majority of cases. However, some of the items will apply to only the occasional divorce and child support case. Briefly, the most common documents that should be requested in ordinary family law cases include:

- Personal income tax returns (including copies of W-2s, 1099s, K-1s, and other supporting documents and schedules)
- Pay statements or stubs (showing current and year-to-date wages, bonuses, commissions, overtime, retirement contributions, and other pay or benefits)
- Personal financial statements
- Loan applications (for mortgages, home equity lines of credit, credit cards, auto loans, or other personal or business loans)
- Documentation of debts (loan agreements and receipts related to any personal loans from financial institutions, individuals, or any company)
- Insurance documents (proof of coverage, declaration pages, policy documents, asset listings, appraisals, invoices, or billing statements)
- Real estate documents (tax bills, closing statements, deeds, appraisals, mortgages, or leases)

- Personal property documents (documentation for significant assets, including invoices, receipts, appraisals, titles, loan applications, registrations, and photographs)
- Wills, living wills, powers of attorney, and trust documents
- Inventory of safes and safe deposit boxes
- Bank statements, deposit tickets, canceled checks, and check registers (including checking accounts, money markets, and savings accounts)
- Brokerage account statements (all accounts including those owned individually, jointly, as trustee, or as guardian)
- Retirement account statements (IRA, 401(k), 403(b), pension)
- Credit card statements
- Copies of personal finance software data (Quicken, QuickBooks, or something similar)

For family law cases including business interests, the most common documents to request include:

- Business ownership records (stock certificates, charters, operating agreements, joint venture agreements, corporate minutes, or other related documents)
- Business income tax returns (Form 1065, 1120, or 1120S) for any business in which the spouse/parent has had an ownership interest for the last five years
- Business financial statements (including profit and loss statements, balance sheets, and statements of cash flow) for the last five years
- Books of minutes for companies controlled directly or indirectly by the party, including articles of incorporation, amendments, bylaws, minutes, and resolutions of shareholders and directors

In addition, many other detailed accounting documents related to the business ventures might be requested. These are enumerated in Appendix B and are more thoroughly discussed in Chapter 12.

What is the importance of these documents? A brief summary of the documents follows; in Chapter 10, we will discuss in greater detail the information found in the documents.

- Income tax returns summarize the income of the parties prior to the divorce and can point to ownership of certain assets, such as real estate, investment accounts, or business interests.
- Bank, brokerage, and credit card statements show the details of income and expenditures and may help identify assets, uncover unusual spending, or find previously undisclosed sources of income.
- Insurance policies can help identify valuable assets such as jewelry, art, automobiles, boats, and the like.

Depending on the circumstances of the family law case, there is no limit to the creativity that may be used to uncover the truth about the finances. Valuable records may include medical records, telephone records, shipping records, e-mails, photographs, calendars, and social media postings. Specialized software or applications ("apps") may be used to conduct personal financial matters or business transactions, and data from those may be important as well.

Even though financial documents can be obtained with discovery demands and subpoenas, it is often much easier for a spouse with access to the documents to simply copy or retain them. Being proactive in gathering financial documentation can save time and may prevent the destruction of important items.

If hard copies of documents are available to the spouse at the home or an office (to which the spouse has legitimate access), the spouse should copy or secure them. If information is available online and the spouse has legitimate access to that data, it should be downloaded and printed for all available periods. While gathering these documents may be tedious and time-consuming, immediate access to financial documents (rather than waiting for the documents to be produced during discovery) can provide a significant advantage in the litigation.

The expertise of the forensic accountant should be used to the maximum extent during discovery to ensure complete disclosure by the other side. The forensic accountant can help craft demands for documents and interrogatories. If the attorney attempts to do financial discovery alone, he or she runs the risk of poorly worded demands that use improper terminology for various accounting and financial documents. The improper terminology may inadvertently offer the other side some latitude to not disclose important documents and information.

Demands should not only specifically identify the documents demanded but also include more general language to ensure that the items are produced. For example, a specific demand would ask for an aged accounts receivable report, and the more general description would request any documents summarizing the amounts owed by each customer and the dates those amounts were invoiced. If the company does not call their report an "aged accounts receivable report," they are still on notice that the demand is for a report showing customer balances and how old those balances are.

The financial expert should review documents and responses received in discovery to determine whether they meet the demands. If they do not, the expert can help craft follow-up demands and interrogatories. When doing a lifestyle analysis, half the battle is getting the right documents. The forensic accountant should play an active role in this process to ensure that all necessary documentation is received.

Time Period Analyzed

One of the key considerations when beginning a lifestyle analysis is the time period to analyze. It is common to analyze data for three to five years prior to separation. This length of time often provides enough history to see a fair representation of historical income and expenses and to reliably predict future income and expenses. With a longer timeframe, it is sometimes easier to see unusual items that may need to be adjusted, and the "normal" income and expenses may be easier to identify. That is not to say that an analysis over a shorter period will not be accurate or useful. Depending on the circumstances, analyzing two years may provide enough information for the financial expert.

To limit the cost and scope of the work, financial experts will sometimes restrict the analysis to a period of one year prior to separation. However, this makes it difficult to tell whether there are unusual items included in that period. One year of data may not be enough to establish a solid history and pattern of spending, but an analysis of a short period of time should not immediately be dismissed as useless or unreliable. Ideally a one-year analysis would only be used in cases with severe budgetary concerns or another compelling reason.

The financial expert may be asked to summarize the lifestyle analysis in one or more of the following ways:

- Pre-separation
- Post-separation up to divorce
- Post-divorce projected need

It is important for the forensic accountant to be able to present results for these different time periods, even if not initially asked to do so. Needs can change as the family law case progresses, and it is important that the expert be flexible in fulfilling those needs. If a database of transactions is put together right away, the financial expert should be able to summarize the information in multiple different ways as the need arises.

Document Management

In family law cases with large volumes of documents, it is essential to have them well organized and catalogued. This is necessary so missing documents can be identified and important documents can be found at a moment's notice.

The best way to track documents received is with a document log that lists monthly and annual documents that are to be produced in a chart like the one on page 88. Fields on the chart may include institution name, account number (typically the last four digits only), type of account, or name on the account. The aim is to create a chart that gives critical information about the document production at a glance.

An X is placed in a box when that document is received. Boxes without Xs can be highlighted in a color such as red to create a quick visual aid for the judge. A chart with a lot of red indicates that many documents have not been produced in discovery, and this can be a powerful tool to demonstrate the noncompliance of the opposing spouse. For example, one spouse may argue that he has produced several boxes of documents and he cannot understand why the other side continues to ask for more. The chart on the next page quickly demonstrates to the judge that even though many bank and credit card statements were produced, there are still substantial gaps in the discovery.

Boxes may also be shaded in gray or some other color if no document is available for that month. For example, if an account was opened midway through the period reflected on the chart, there would be no statements for the early months and those boxes would be shaded gray. Symbols may be used to indicate things like missing pages from a statement. If one account had a change in account number, both the old and new account number should be noted on the chart.

File Maintenance

The testifying financial expert will be required to produce his or her file materials to opposing counsel, so it is important to maintain an organized and controlled file. In addition to tracking documents received, the documents should be organized in a way that is most useful to the forensic accountant. Documents will likely be separated by account number or entity and then put in chronological order.

It may be helpful for the expert to create a key documents file in which copies of the most important or most frequently referenced documents are kept for easy access. Documents that are received during discovery but deemed irrelevant should be set aside, not discarded. In the event that those documents are later deemed relevant, they may be retrieved and used.

What about the financial expert who claims that he or she has no file? Statements like that are not credible, especially in larger cases. The forensic accountant ought to have documents, correspondence, court filings, and miscellaneous calculations in a file. It is common for experts to limit the notes taken or extraneous documents included in the file, but it is unusual to have no file, so that claim should be viewed skeptically.

Document Inventory
James and Amanda Copeland

Institution	Type	Name on Acct	No.	2018 Jan	Feb	Mar	Apr	May	Jun	Jul	Aug	Sep	Oct	Nov	Dec	2019 Jan	Feb	Mar	Apr	May	Jun	Jul	Aug	Sep	Oct	Nov	Dec
AMEX	CC	James	26005	×	×	×	×	×	×	×	×	×	×	×	×	×	×	×	×	×	×	×	×	M	M	M	M
BOA	Bank	James	1663	×	×	×	×	×	×	×	×	×	×	×	×	×	×	×	×	×	×	×	×	×	×	×	×
BOA	Bank	James & Amanda	6821	×	×	×	×	×	×	×	×	×	×	×	×	×	×	×	×	×	×	A	A	A	A	A	A
BOA	Bank	Amanda	3864	×	×	×	×	×	M	M	M	M	M	M	×	×	×	×	×	×	×	A	A	A	A	A	A
BOA	CC	James	1118	•	•	•	•	•	•	•	•	•	•	•	•	•	•	•	•	•	•	•	•	•	•	•	•
BOA	CC	James	7591	×	×	×	×	×	×	×	×	×	×	×	×	×	×	×	×	×	×	×	×	×	×	×	×
BOA	CC	Amanda	2495	×	×	×	×	×	×	×	×	×	×	×	×	×	×	×	×	×	×	×	×	×	×	×	×
Chase	Bank	Copeland Co.	0605	×	×	×	×	×	×	×	×	×	×	×	×	×	×	×	×	×	×	×	×	A	A	A	A
Chase United	Bank	James	1847	M	M	M	M	M	×	×	×	×	×	×	×	×	×	×	×	×	×	×	×	×	×	×	×
Chase United	Bank	Copeland Co.	2277	×	×	×	×	×	×	×	×	×	×	×	×	×	×	×	×	×	×	×	×	×	×	×	×
US Bank	Bank	Copeland Co.	4109	×	×	×	×	×	×	×	×	×	×	×	×	×	×	×	×	×	×	×	×	×	×	×	×

• No activity

Account not open (A)

Missing statement (M)

When an expert's file is requested or subpoenaed by opposing counsel, the expert should consult with retaining counsel about the specifics related to the production. Retaining counsel may want to review the file materials before they are produced and may have a preferred process for the production.

Failure to Produce Documents

It can be frustrating to repeatedly demand or subpoena documents during discovery and fail to get them in whole or in part. Family lawyers should be careful not to accept claims that "most" of the documents were produced, especially when the documents in question include bank statements, brokerage statements, and credit card statements.

Even *one* missing page or statement could dramatically affect the case. That one page or statement could contain a transaction that is the key to discovering previously unknown assets or sources of income. That page or statement could prove that a party to the divorce was hiding assets or moving money in a way that is meant to deprive his or her spouse of a rightful share of it. While estimates can be made for missing data, there is a risk in doing so.

If there is difficulty getting copies of individual or business income tax returns, they can be requested directly from the Internal Revenue Service using Form 4506, Request for Copy of Tax Return. This requires the signature of the individual or someone authorized to request the tax returns on behalf of a company. The fee is $50 per return, and returns up to six years old can be requested. It may take up to 75 days to receive the tax returns.

If tax return information is needed quicker, Form 4506-T, Request for Transcript of Tax Return, may be used for personal income tax returns only. This form can be used to request tax return transcripts, tax account information, W-2 information, 1099 information, verification of nonfiling, or records of a taxpayer's account. Transcripts can also be accessed online by the taxpayer after passing an identity verification process. There is no cost to get a transcript, but the transcripts only go back three years and do not reflect any amended returns or adjustments made by the Internal Revenue Service.

When a closely held business is part of the marital estate, there are sometimes problems getting financial documents related to the business. The spouse who controls the business may say that the accounting records and income tax returns are confidential and cannot be disclosed during the divorce. A spouse may claim that the board of directors needs to approve any dissemination of financial documents.

These arguments are not true. The Internal Revenue Code (Section 6103) specifically allows access to income tax returns of a company for:

- Anyone who was a member of a partnership during the tax year
- Any shareholder of a corporation with a 1 percent or greater interest

If the company refuses to produce the tax return or other financial information, the attorney could ask the court to order the documents to be produced or could submit a written request to the Internal Revenue Service. Alternatively, a subpoena to the company's accounting firm should cause the income tax returns and other financial documents to be produced.

One other hurdle during discovery may be a claim that since the company produced income tax returns, there is no need to produce financial statements, or vice versa. This argument is invalid. Income tax returns and financial statements provide different information, so both are needed to do a complete analysis of the business. Sometimes a judge will not order that both be produced, suggesting one or the other is not useful or that the information contained in them is redundant. If both are necessary to the analysis, the financial expert should help explain specifically why both are important.

A business owner may alternatively claim that the business tax return is not needed by opposing counsel, since the owner produced his or her K-1 from the business. A K-1 provides very little information about the finances of the business, so it is insufficient to analyze the company. The income tax return must be produced so the expert can do a thorough examination of the business.

Depositions

The forensic accountant may assist counsel with preparing for depositions. Lines of questioning relative to financial matters can be developed in conjunction with expected responses and potential follow-up questions. The financial expert can assist with depositions of a number of parties: the spouse, the other side's financial expert witness, accountants working for the individuals or relevant companies, or any witness who will be testifying about financial matters. Most family lawyers do not have strong financial backgrounds, so preparing the attorney for the deposition of a witness can be as important as the deposition itself.

The preparation should include:

- Educating the attorney on the background of the financial issues and the most important details
- Developing lines of questioning
- Providing the attorney with common names for financial documents and reports
- Helping the attorney use the correct terminology when speaking about accounting or financial issues
- Discussing expected answers during the deposition and preparing follow-up questions

Sometimes the financial expert is asked to attend the depositions of people who will testify about financial matters. This can be advantageous for the family lawyer, since the expert can suggest questions to ask based on responses to other questions in the deposition. This may be done by providing notes to the attorney during the deposition, or through discussions between the attorney and the expert during breaks. If the expert does not attend the deposition, he or she is left to read transcripts later and tell the attorney that certain questions ought to have been asked or suggest other necessary follow-up discovery.

Chapter 6

Documents Used in the Lifestyle Analysis

In this chapter we discuss the documents needed to perform a lifestyle analysis and how those documents are used. We have already talked generally about financial documents that are used in divorce and child support cases, but here we will talk about their relevance to the lifestyle analysis. In later chapters, we will focus on specific types of income or assets and, more specifically, how the documents are used to investigate those items.

This book does not discuss the basics of accounting, as our focus is very narrow and our space is limited. It assumes you have a basic working knowledge of income taxes, financial statements, and accounting terminology. Miles Mason, Sr., JD, CPA, covers the topic of accounting for lawyers thoroughly in *The Forensic Accounting Deskbook*. An entire chapter is devoted to discussing financial statements, basis of accounting, general ledgers, and audits. Mr. Mason's book covers all sorts of information on working with financial experts and dealing with financial issues in divorce, and it is an invaluable reference tool for family lawyers.

Following are some of the most common financial documents utilized in family law cases, with a discussion of information they can provide about income, assets, liabilities, and expenditures.

Income Tax Returns, W-2s, and Current Pay Stubs

An individual's income tax returns (Form 1040), W-2s, and current pay stubs are the most common and basic documents evidencing income. Included in Appendix A is a sample of a 2017 personal income tax return (Form 1040) and a sample of the 2018 form along with Schedule 1 and Schedule A (itemized deductions). You may notice that the line numbers on the new Schedule 1 correlate to the line numbers on the old Form 1040, presumably to reduce confusion. The forms changed when the Tax Cuts and Jobs Act of 2017 went into effect, but nearly all of the same information is being captured in the income tax filings as before.

The income tax return will provide information on the following sources of income. This list includes some pointers on ways the items can be analyzed to search for hidden income and hidden assets.

- Wages—The figures reported on the income tax return should be matched to the W-2. The W-2 and the pay stubs provide additional information on the employers, pay rates, total pay, retirement account contributions, certain benefits, and taxes withheld. It is important to determine whether the wages reported on the W-2 are truly gross wages, or if the wages have been reduced by retirement contributions. If retirement contributions were subtracted to arrive at gross wages on the W-2, it is important to do the math to arrive at the actual gross income prior to any deductions. Additional analysis may include tracing bank deposits to ensure that all wages were used for the benefit of the family.
- Taxable interest and tax-exempt interest—These items of income must be considered when calculating income available for support. They are also important because they can point to bank, investment, and brokerage accounts that may not have been specifically disclosed in the family law case.
- Dividends—Like interest, dividends must be considered in calculations of income available for support and can point to bank, investment, and brokerage accounts that may not have been disclosed.

- IRAs, pensions, annuities—Any activity on this line should be evaluated to determine if all retirement accounts have been disclosed and considered.
- Social Security benefits—Two figures are reported for Social Security, the total amount received and the taxable amount. The total amount received is the important figure for an analysis of income.
- Taxable refunds or credits—Refunds should be examined to determine if they were shared by the parties, and the expert should evaluate whether a spouse is having unusually large amounts withheld from paychecks. This could be a technique used to hide funds until after the divorce is final.
- Alimony received—This item relates to a prior marriage and will likely not be a factor in the current marriage and divorce.
- Business income or loss—Income on this line comes from Schedule C, which form shows income or loss from a sole proprietorship or single-member limited liability company (LLC). Chapter 12 covers the business lifestyle analysis, so information on this line item will be found there.
- Capital gains or losses—Along with interest and dividends mentioned previously, this portion of the income tax return can point to assets in investment and brokerage accounts. Information on this line is from Schedule D.
- Other gains or losses—This line item often relates to sales of property used in business, so it should be evaluated to determine if other assets or income streams exist. Income on this line can come from several different schedules.
- Rental real estate, royalties, partnerships, S corporations, trusts—These items should be investigated in the same way as many business interests. Refer to Chapter 12 for information regarding the business lifestyle analysis.
- Farm income or loss—This item is also a business interest that should be investigated using the methods detailed in Chapter 12.
- Unemployment compensation—Information about unemployment benefits should be used in conjunction with wage information to determine if all of the income benefitted the family.

- Other income—Many types of income could fall under this category, so any income reported on this line on the income tax return should be carefully evaluated. Schedules and attachments to the income tax return will indicate what the income is.

The personal income tax returns can also be useful when quantifying the spending of the family for the lifestyle analysis. The items of most interest include the following items from Schedule A:

- Mortgage interest deduction—This item helps verify real estate owned (the asset side) and loans outstanding (the liability side). It also helps the financial expert calculate an estimated monthly payment.
- State and local income tax deduction—The accounting expert may match this deduction to the underlying accounting records. Be aware that starting in 2018, this deduction is limited to $10,000. The deduction should be evaluated to determine if it is excessive and/or used to hide cash until the divorce is complete.
- Real estate tax deduction—Similar to mortgage interest, the real estate tax deduction points to the ownership of real estate.

Income tax returns can be audited, amended, or both audited and amended. The taxing authorities can also send a notice to the taxpayer indicating an error or omission in the tax return and an underpayment or overpayment of taxes. The family law attorney should inquire as to whether any of these have happened and request documentation of the notices, audit results, and/or amended income tax return. Inquiries should also be made about whether there are any unpaid taxes, interest, and penalties or any existing tax liens.

In addition to the income tax return itself, the 1099s that were used to help prepare the tax return can provide useful information. The 1099s are issued for items such as rent, royalties, nonemployee compensation (subcontractor or self-employed income), fees received by an attorney, dividends, interest, government payments, and a variety of other kinds of income. The 1099s might provide information on real estate or other valuable assets owned, investment accounts, the activity within the accounts, and the account balances.

Business Financial Statements

Business financial statements should be evaluated and compared to underlying supporting documentation. Financial statements are typically requested for a period of three to five years before the separation of the spouses, but a longer period may be requested if a larger picture of the business is desired. Yearly data should be compared for the period under review to determine any significant changes in income, expenses, assets, or liabilities between years and to discover if there is any trend established. Monthly or quarterly data may provide more insight into the operations and how income is earned and expenses are incurred throughout the year. The analysis of business finances will be discussed thoroughly in Chapter 12.

Appendix B is a list of financial items that may be requested during the discovery portion of a family law case. The following documents may be requested for use in the analysis of business finances:

- Copies of valuations or appraisals done within the preceding five years
- Copies of budgets, forecasts, projections, or business plans prepared within the preceding five years
- Copies of all bank statements, checks, deposit slips and deposited items, and wire transfers for the last three years
- Copies of all credit card statements for the last three years
- Copies of all brokerage account statements for the last three years
- Copies of all applications for credit with any financial institution during the preceding three years
- Access to detailed accounting records, including the general ledger, general journal, sales journal, purchases journal, cash receipts journal, cash disbursements journal, and subsidiary ledgers

The financial statements are used to determine the profitability, assets, and liabilities of a business. It is important to note that because of differences in accounting rules and tax laws, numbers may differ between the financial statements and income tax returns. However, any differences noted should be evaluated to determine if they are simply a result of specifics of the tax code, or if there is a different reason.

Information found in the financial statements includes the following items, along with questions or considerations that may pertain to each:

- Assets of the business—Are there assets? What kind of assets (fixed assets like buildings and equipment or intangible assets such as patents or goodwill)? Have they been depreciated (fixed assets) or amortized (intangible assets)? Does depreciation or amortization need to be adjusted for a business valuation or support calculation?
- Liabilities of the business—How much does the business owe and to whom? What were the borrowed funds used for: purchase of assets, operations, payment of dividends or distributions to owners, or something else?
- Income—Has the income been going up or down? How are the changes in income explained? Could income be manipulated to affect calculations in the divorce? Income changes between periods should be analyzed in terms of both dollar changes and percent changes.
- Expenses—Have business expenses been increasing or decreasing? How are the changes explained? Have market conditions played a role? Are there other explanations? Could expenses be manipulated to affect divorce calculations? Evaluate changes between periods in terms of dollar changes and percent changes.
- Ownership—Has the ownership of the company changed? Could the change have anything to do with the divorce? Was any change in ownership done through an arm's-length sale at market prices?
- Compensation—Has there been any unusual change in the owner's compensation? Is the change related to known changes in business operations or market conditions? Have cash withdrawals been made outside of normal compensation? For example, has the owner withdrawn cash from his or her capital account? Is there an apparent attempt to influence support calculations? Does compensation need to be adjusted for purposes of a business valuation?
- Benefits—Are there any major changes in nonwage compensation and benefits? Should the benefits or perks be considered in support calculations or business valuations?

A detailed analysis of financial statements should be done around the time of separation. The analysis could show a company's expenses remained constant, while reported income fell dramatically. This would be unusual. A decrease in income with no related decrease in expenses (especially in a period that coincides with a divorce action) may indicate that the business owner is intentionally underreporting income.

Even though it is most typical to analyze annual financial statements, monthly or quarterly statements can be even more important. There may be seasonality to a business, and the monthly or quarterly financial statements will provide insight into this. In addition, in-house or external accountants often make adjustments to the financial statements at year-end. Monthly or quarterly statements will show you unadjusted numbers for the earlier months or quarters of the year, and there could be valuable information gleaned from those numbers. Look for inconsistencies in numbers across the months or quarters and determine if any of the year-end adjustments were made for the purpose of manipulating figures for the divorce.

Detailed information on investigating business interests is in Chapter 12. There we discuss evaluating individual line items in the financial statements.

Business Budgets or Projections

Budgets and projections are difficult to rely on because their accuracy is unknown. However, they can still provide information on assets, income, customers, expenses, and vendors that may need investigation. If the actual results are far out of line with the budgets or projections, the reasons should be investigated.

Business Accounting Records

Detailed accounting records, including the general ledger and supporting documentation, may be useful in analyzing income and expenses of the business. This will be discussed in detail in Chapter 12.

Personal Accounting Records

Individuals may keep handwritten check registers or utilize personal finance software to track their personal spending. It is important to review the records kept by the spouses to understand how the family classified expenditures. Remember that the records kept by the spouses may not be accurate (through either error or deliberate manipulation), so any reliance on the check register or data within personal finance software should be thoughtfully considered.

Bank Statements and Related Documents

Bank statements, along with the related checks and deposit tickets, are very reliable sources of information because the documents come from a disinterested third party. A bank (especially one in the United States) often has no interest in manipulating documents and account balances. Therefore, as a general rule, bank statements and related documents can be relied on as an accurate source for the truth about where money came from or went.

Ensure that *all* known bank accounts are analyzed. If any accounts are missing from the analysis, there is a risk that important details may be hidden. Investigating the details of transactions in known bank accounts may uncover clues to undisclosed accounts. Both inflows and outflows from the bank account should be examined. Bank deposits and expenditures should be compared to financial disclosures and income tax returns for discrepancies.

- Confirm or refute claimed income. Deposits from previously unidentified sources could constitute income that should be considered in the divorce. They may also point to assets that should be divided.
- Evaluate expenditures to determine if they exceed the disclosed income. If so, try to determine how the excess expenditures were funded. This may lead to the discovery of a previously undisclosed source of income.
- Determine whether all disclosed income was deposited into known bank accounts. If it was not, investigate whether other accounts exist, and whether they may be part of the marital estate.

- Find checks or electronic transfers of funds to previously unknown accounts, entities, or individuals. This money trail may lead to other accounts, which could lead to other assets such as automobiles and real estate. It could also be evidence of dissipation or waste of marital assets.

Brokerage Statements

Similar to the bank documents, the expert should examine the brokerage and investment account statements. Incoming funds should be traced to sources of income or transfers from other known accounts. Withdrawals from the brokerage accounts should be examined, and the accumulation of assets in these accounts may be very material to the property division.

Credit Card Statements

Because credit cards are so heavily used by consumers, the account statements can yield substantial information for the lifestyle analysis. Not only do the credit card records detail the spending, the statements may also provide evidence of dissipation or waste of marital assets. For example, dates of transactions may be important to verify the whereabouts of the parties on certain dates, and detailed information such as names on airline tickets can provide additional clues about spending.

Loan Applications

One of the most valuable tools when analyzing personal and business finances can be loan applications. Applications for home mortgages, automobile loans or leases, equipment leases or loans, personal loans, or other commercial loans require the borrower to disclose detailed financial information. The borrower must typically disclose assets, liabilities, and income sources, and these disclosures should be compared to disclosures in the family law case to determine if there are any significant discrepancies.

Borrowers tend to be very candid about their income and assets when applying for loans because they want to make an excellent case for receiving funds from the lender. Assets and income tend to be fully disclosed in loan applications (because higher income and assets will help secure the loan), whereas disclosures during divorce are more likely to exclude some of the income and assets (to deprive the spouse of a share of the income and assets).

The loan application may be used to impeach a spouse if the disclosures during divorce differ substantially from disclosures in the loan application. Opposing counsel will likely argue that the loan application should not be considered in the divorce because it was prepared for a different, unrelated purpose. Counsel may further argue that the numbers differ from divorce-related disclosures not because either is untruthful but because of a myriad of unusual reasons. These arguments can be combatted with common sense. The values should not differ between the divorce disclosure and the loan application, and any difference must mean that the applicant is lying either to the lender or to the family court. Remember, too, that loans are often securitized with assets, and documents regarding the secured assets should be evaluated to determine if the assets belong in the marital estate.

Bankruptcy Court Documents

Personal and business bankruptcies require substantial disclosure of financial details. Bankruptcy court documents should be evaluated and compared to tax returns, financial disclosures, and related financial information produced in the divorce.

Other Miscellaneous Documents

Sometimes the primary documents discussed above simply are not available during a divorce. That is the time to get creative and think of other documents that could provide useful information. The financial expert will likely need to estimate certain items within the family's lifestyle. Documents that evidence housing costs (mortgage, real estate, utilities, etc.), transportation costs, and other typical items may help the expert estimate monthly expenses. In addition, third-party guidance may help establish reasonable estimates.

One source of data for typical family expenses is the Internal Revenue Service, which publishes national standards for food, housekeeping supplies, apparel and services, personal care products and services, and miscellaneous other items. The national standards for allowable living expenses quantify monthly expenses for families of one to four people, and the figures are updated periodically. A recent example is included in Appendix C. These figures may be used to estimate reasonable costs for a typical family in the absence of other information.

What Is Proof?

Much of the lifestyle analysis will be completed using documents that come from third parties, such as banks, brokerages, and credit card companies. As mentioned previously, third-party documents are considered to be very reliable. That is, they are generally not subject to manipulation.

Documents prepared by a spouse, such as a check register, can say whatever the spouse wants them to say. On the other hand, bank documents tell you exactly where the money originated or ended. The spouse may be able to write a phony memo on a check, but the bank documents will confirm beyond a shadow of a doubt who received the money.

Not all financial documents are of the same value to the case. The financial investigator must very carefully consider the source of the documents before determining how much to rely on them.

Chapter 7

Financial Analysis of Documents

In Chapter 5 and Appendix B, we discuss a lengthy list of financial documents that can be requested or subpoenaed in a family law case. These documents are aimed at identifying assets and liabilities, determining income, and evaluating expenditures.

In many divorce cases, it is easy to determine income and identify assets and liabilities. In a run-of-the-mill case, income includes W-2 wages of the spouses and a few small items such as interest income and dividends. Assets and liabilities are obvious, as they often include houses, automobiles, and a bank account or two.

In other divorce cases, it is much more complicated. Divorces involving self-employed individuals, rental properties, income-producing assets, or high-level executives with special perks and benefits are more difficult to evaluate. These are the cases in which more documentation must be evaluated, including the laundry list of documents in Appendix B and possibly other documents depending on the unique factors in the family law case.

General Procedures

How does the financial expert evaluate the data and documents received during the discovery portion of a family law case? In general, the following procedures should be performed:

1. Complete a document inventory (discussed in Chapter 5).
2. Get a general overview of the case by reading the pleadings and answers to interrogatories. Discuss with the client the high points of the financial portion of the case to get an understanding of the potential issues.
3. Perform a high-level review of the financial documents. This may include a brief analysis of income tax returns and financial statements to become familiar with the financial situation. It may also include searching for red flags that could point to fraud or the need for a lifestyle analysis.
4. Analyze historical income, looking for changes and trends in the income and identifying explanations for them.
5. Determine if an analysis of expenditures is necessary to the case. This may be necessary to prepare a budget, evaluate the need for support, or quantify the lifestyle of the parties before or after separation.
6. Evaluate income and/or expenses using the procedures detailed throughout the rest of this book.

Determining Income

When attempting to calculate the income of the spouse or spouses, it is important to remember that income is not determined simply on the basis of historical earnings. It is necessary to also consider the future prospects for income and how the income scenario may change after the divorce. For example, one of the spouses may encounter a job change with a related change in earnings. Even if a change is not a result of a divorce, it still must be considered, as changes in earnings may change a spouse's ability to pay support.

In evaluating historical income, it is necessary to consider whether historical income was abnormally high or low for some reason. For example, suppose a business run by the spouse had lower net income in the past because there was a substantial investment to increase the capacity of the business. The investment included operating expenses and depreciation of fixed assets, which lowered historical earnings but created an opportunity for the company to generate higher income in the future. Thus, the projection of future earnings must not rely solely on the historical earnings but must consider the future prospects for income.

Of course, it is also important to consider whether one or both of the spouses has intentionally manipulated or decreased income in anticipation of divorce. This is not the same thing as hiding income or assets. Instead, this refers to the manipulation of a known income stream. For example, a law firm partner may temporarily, purposely decrease his salary to manipulate his income for support calculations. The intention would likely be to restore the salary sometime after the family law case concludes. A salesperson may ask the employer to temporarily suspend commission payouts. A manager may ask to have a bonus delayed until after the divorce is over.

Another common issue is the spouse who is accused of not working at full capacity. An allegation may be made that he or she has the ability to earn a greater income if employed at a different job or working longer hours. A spouse may attempt early retirement or semi-retirement to avoid having earnings that are subject to a support order. A parent may have marketable skills in a field that has lots of job openings, but he or she may need to be home with children part-time or full-time, impacting the earnings. Sometimes earning capacity must be factored into support calculations related to the lifestyle analysis.

Income for the purpose of family law proceedings can be calculated in one of four ways. These four methods have been developed for use by the Internal Revenue Service in calculating unreported income in tax cases. Because these methods are routinely used by the Internal Revenue Service in civil and criminal income tax cases, they are considered reliable when done properly. The four primary methods for completing a lifestyle analysis are:

- Specific items method—Transaction details are analyzed to identify specific items of income. Documents for known bank, brokerage, investment, and credit card accounts are examined to identify sources of funds. The detailed transactions from the statements are analyzed, categorized, and summarized. The data is accumulated in a spreadsheet or database so that it can be quickly sorted, summed, and subtotaled to provide insight into the data.

- Bank deposits method—All bank deposits are summed, adjusting the total to remove deposits that are transfers from other accounts or deposits from sources that do not represent income. The total of the bank deposits (less transfers between accounts and sources that are not income) may represent the total income of the party.
- Expenditures method—Bank, brokerage, investment, and credit card account documents are examined to identify uses of funds, also called expenditures. The detailed transactions from the statements are analyzed, categorized, and summarized in the same way as the specific items method. Expenditures are accumulated, and the expert determines the level of income that is required to fund those expenditures, taking into consideration income taxes. If known sources of income are not sufficient to pay the expenses, the financial expert must consider whether undisclosed sources of income exist.
- Net worth method—This analysis evaluates the change in an individual's net worth and compares it to the known sources of income and the known expenditures. If the net worth increases beyond what is expected based on known sources of income, this may indicate unreported income. The net worth method is used by the government in criminal cases to calculate unreported income, so it is known to be reliable if done correctly.

The Lifestyle Analysis

Specific Items Method

One of the most straightforward ways to complete a lifestyle analysis is through an analysis of specific items of income. This method is possible when there are substantial documents detailing cash inflows. The specific items method is considered a direct method of verifying income.

Income-related information is gathered from bank and brokerage statements, tax-related documents, and business records. Inflows are identified and summed, theoretically verifying the income disclosed in the family law case. For example, the income of a dental practice may be verified by examining documents such as income tax returns, bank statements, and billing records. Theoretically, all three of these items should reconcile to one another to verify the income of the business. Other records of the business, such as appointment logs and insurance submissions, may also help validate income numbers.

The specific items method is easy to comprehend and present, which makes it an attractive option for evaluating claimed income. We must assume that judges and juries have no accounting background and need the numbers simplified. With this method, the court will easily be able to understand how income was calculated.

However, the specific items method is rarely used effectively in a family law case when looking for income. If a lifestyle analysis is done to calculate income, it is typically because it has been difficult or impossible to verify the party's income. Presumably, documentation verifying income does not exist or has not been produced. Without such documentation, a specific items analysis cannot be accurately completed.

Occasionally, documentation evidencing hidden sources of income is acquired, and in that case the specific items method may be viable. In other words, once documentation related to concealed income is uncovered, that documentation may make it possible to complete this direct method of calculating income.

Bank Deposits Method

The bank deposits method is an indirect method of proving income. Income is reconstructed by adding up bank deposits made by the spouse. This method relies on the spouse making regular deposits into a business or personal bank account and depositing all sources of income to the bank.

Like the specific items method, the bank deposits method can rarely be used successfully in the family law case to determine income. Spouses who intend to hide income will likely not deposit all income to known bank accounts. They may deposit funds to hidden accounts, either in their names or in the names of other individuals or entities, or they may avoid depositing funds altogether.

A detailed analysis of bank deposits can be used in other ways, however. In one case the bank deposits method was used to uncover $150,000 that should have been deposited to the family bank account but was not. The husband had an ownership interest in six business entities, with wages being paid to him from two of them and distributions of profits from all of them. The wife was concerned whether all wages and profits were deposited to family bank accounts. She was further concerned whether her husband was owed distributions from any of the entities but was potentially avoiding taking the distributions until after the divorce was completed.

The tax returns and financial statements of each entity were examined to determine how much was distributed to the husband. This data was compared to personal bank statements and no discrepancies were found. This did not give a complete picture, however.

It was necessary to dig into the detailed accounting records of the entities to see specific instances of funds paid to the husband. While the income tax returns and financial statements easily show certain payments and distributions, there was more detail needed. The general ledger of each business was analyzed, searching for any payments made to the husband. This labor-intensive process paid off. $150,000 in expense reimbursement checks that were paid to the husband but never deposited into the family's bank account were found. If it is assumed the wife is entitled to half of that asset, the $75,000 value to her in the divorce more than paid for the professional fees for the investigation.

Expenditures Method

The expenditures method of calculating income involves analyzing and tabulating expenditures to determine the total income that would be required to fund them. Expenditures are extracted from bank, brokerage, and credit card statements. Each expenditure for the period under review must be captured from the statements and categorized so that totals can be accumulated for the period under analysis.

For example, expenses could be put into such categories as mortgage payment, automobile lease, utilities, groceries, and clothing. Use the categories identified on your state's financial disclosure form as a guide to important categories for the classification of expenses.

In addition to classifying expenses, the forensic accountant may also allocate expenses to family members. This includes the husband, wife, and children, but it may also include extended family if the married couple was funding some of the extended family's living expenses. For example, school tuition and extracurricular activities are for the benefit of the children, so those expenses should be assigned to the children so they may be treated properly when calculating child support.

After the individual transactions are categorized and allocated to family members, evaluate total spending by category for relevant periods to analyze historical spending and develop projections of expenses for future periods. Calculate the income necessary to fund those expenditures and compare this figure to the income reported to determine if there are discrepancies. If the reported income is substantially less than the income necessary to fund the expenses, there could be unreported sources of income.

Net Worth Method

The net worth method of proof follows a methodology similar to the expenditures method because the change in net worth must be evaluated in conjunction with expenditures during the period. The expenditures method will likely be incorporated into the net worth analysis, because it is necessary to know the spending of the parties during the period under analysis, so a detailed analysis of spending will be necessary.

The net worth of the parties is determined by subtracting known liabilities from known assets. If the parties earn more money than they spend in a period, the net worth should increase during that period. Conversely, if the parties are spending more than they are making (usually by incurring debt), the net worth will decrease during the period.

This net worth method is completed as follows:

1. Calculate ending net worth by identifying assets (at the cost to purchase them) and liabilities at the end of the period under analysis. Liabilities are subtracted from assets to arrive at net worth. An accurate net worth is critical to the analysis.
2. Calculate beginning net worth by identifying the assets and liabilities at the beginning of the period under analysis. Liabilities are again subtracted from assets to arrive at net worth.

3. Subtract beginning net worth from ending net worth to arrive at the change in net worth. A positive number indicates the net worth has increased. A negative number indicates the net worth has decreased.
4. Analyze expenditures during the period. These include all living expenses, asset purchases, asset sales, additional debts incurred, debts paid down, or other inflows or outflows of funds.
5. Add outflows of funds calculated in step 4 to the change in net worth calculated in step 3.
6. Subtract inflows of funds other than income (e.g., gifts received) from the change in net worth calculated in step 3.
7. The resulting figure is the calculated gross income necessary to achieve the change in net worth, which is essentially the money it takes to fund the lifestyle.
8. Compare the calculated gross income to the reported gross income. Any difference may represent unreported income.

The calculation can be summarized this way:

	Ending assets
–	Ending liabilities
=	Ending net worth
–	Beginning net worth
=	Increase or (decrease) in net worth
+	Expenditures (living expenses, asset purchases, etc.)
–	Inflows of funds other than income
=	Income necessary to fund lifestyle

Let's assume that at the end of 2018, the spouse had assets of $12,000,000 and liabilities of $3,000,000. The prior year, the assets were $13,000,000 and the liabilities were $5,000,000. The monthly living expenses were $20,000, or $240,000 per year. This figure was derived from a detailed analysis of the expenditures in the financial records. The only known sources of income were the spouse's wages of $500,000 per year and a gift of $10,000 from the spouse's uncle.

The calculation under the net worth method would be done as follows:

	$12,000,000	2018 assets
−	3,000,000	2018 liabilities
=	9,000,000	2018 net worth
−	8,000,000	2017 assets less liabilities
=	1,000,000	Increase in net worth
+	240,000	Annual living expenses
−	10,000	Other sources of funds
=	1,230,000	Income necessary to fund lifestyle

This calculation shows that the spouse would have needed $1,230,000 of income during the year to fund the living expenses and accumulate assets. However, the only income that was disclosed was the wages of $500,000. The difference between the income necessary to fund the lifestyle and the known income is $730,000. This represents potentially undisclosed income, and the forensic accountant will need to determine possible sources for these funds.

Key points in completing a thorough and accurate net worth analysis include the following:

- When hard data is available, actual figures should be used.
- Reasonable estimates should be made when hard data is not available. The estimates should be carefully considered and should be made conservatively.
- All living expenses should be included. Items like housing, groceries, fuel, utilities, and education are important. Other less frequent expenditures must also be considered. This may include vacations, furniture, weddings, or artwork.
- The impact of loans, gifts, and inheritances must be considered. In other words, try to consider all possible inflows of cash that could help explain an increase in net worth that exceeds the known income of the parties.
- The possibility that a party is hoarding cash or other valuable assets must be recognized. If the calculated change in net worth exceeds the

known sources of funds, it is possible that a hidden cash hoard or the sale of hidden assets was used to fund living expenses.

- The financial analyst must be careful not to double-count items. It is especially important that increases in assets or reductions in debts not be duplicated in the tabulation of living expenses.

The net worth method of proof is attractive because it can be used to analyze income and assets even when detailed documentation is not available, either because the opposing spouse is obstructing efforts to get data and documents or because data and documents are legitimately not available. The federal government uses the net worth method of determining income in criminal income tax cases. Because it is accepted in federal criminal cases, family courts often will accept this as a reliable method for calculating income.

There are negatives to using the net worth method of proof, however. First, it can be difficult to understand for someone without an accounting background. It is hoped that the financial expert can effectively explain the technique to non-accountants, but there is always a risk that the court may not understand. Second, opposing counsel will likely argue that the method is unreliable if it includes estimates rather than documented, exact figures.

However, the forensic accountant can (and should) point out that this method was necessitated by the lack of data and documents and was the best alternative. It should be further demonstrated that all estimates were made carefully, and when documentation was available, exact figures were used.

Lifestyle Analysis Software

Forensic accountants have a number of software choices for the lifestyle analysis. The most basic option is a spreadsheet program like Microsoft Excel. Some experts use Quicken personal finance software or QuickBooks small business accounting software. There are various software packages available that attempt to import data from bank, credit card, and investment account statements and put the numbers into a database for the financial investigator. Each of these options has positive and negative aspects.

A simple spreadsheet is easy to populate and manipulate. There is no special knowledge required to use it, so almost anyone can work with a spreadsheet. Transactions can be updated in bulk, saving time over personal finance software packages. On the down side, the data may have to be entered manually into the spreadsheet, and it is easy to make a mistake and corrupt the data. There are no report templates in the spreadsheet program, so any summaries of the data must be created from scratch.

Quicken, QuickBooks, and other financial software packages are fairly easy to use and allow for importing data from financial institutions. However, a fair amount of manual data entry still must be done, and it is a slow process because transactions must be updated individually. It is sometimes difficult to identify which transactions need to be updated. Even though these software packages are ideal for tracking individual or small business finances, they were not developed with litigation in mind, so they do not manage data in a way that works well for lifestyle analysis.

Financial investigation software is often the best way to capture and manipulate data when performing a lifestyle analysis. There are two key functions of such software: capturing financial data and putting it in a database for use in the investigation, and performing analytical procedures on the financial data.

Because financial investigation software was designed for the type of work done in a lifestyle analysis, work can often be completed much faster and more reliably. There is less manual data entry, although there is always some reconciliation and correction that needs to be done, especially if account statements are of questionable quality. Customized software features can increase the accuracy of the data capture and speed up the process of categorizing and analyzing the data. The drawback to this option is that many of the available software packages fall short of their promises. There may be problems with accuracy or with the ability to manipulate data once it is in the database. Cost is another drawback, as this type of software can be very expensive.

Regardless of the software used to complete a lifestyle analysis, the data must be carefully reconciled to underlying documentation to ensure that all transactions are captured and none is duplicated. Data integrity is a critical component of the lifestyle analysis and must be one of the chief concerns.

Conducting Interviews

Inevitably, the data gathered and analyzed raises questions during the course of the financial investigation. The forensic accountant wants to know where money came from, what was bought with funds, why money was moved in a certain way, how accounts are used, and other specifics about the data. Sometimes supporting documentation is provided that answers many of these questions. Often there are numerous questions that aren't answered by other documents produced in the litigation.

The financial expert can certainly interview his or her client. That party likely has some valuable information about income and spending that can be incorporated into the lifestyle analysis. But oftentimes the party who needs the lifestyle analysis is not in a position of power with regard to the finances and therefore does not possess many specifics about transactions.

Good luck getting an interview with the other spouse. Opposing counsel usually has no interest in producing the client to be interviewed. Answers about accounts and transactions often have to be communicated in writing, sometimes formally through interrogatories. This makes the process cumbersome and delays the analysis.

In the event that an interview is permitted, it is important that the investigator be well prepared. This means preparing in advance for questions and a process for reviewing transactions with the interviewee. Volumes have been written on conducting effective interviews, and many training courses are available.

Good interviewers connect well with their subjects, even when the subjects are on the opposite side of a case. Having the right demeanor and body language is a big part of interviewing. Asking questions in an easygoing manner often helps the interview go well, but an attempt to get along with the subject should not overshadow the need to be tough and push for information in certain instances. Being prepared will help the interview go smoothly too, since it is nearly impossible to ask intelligent questions about data with which one is not familiar.

A few general tips for interviewing a party on the opposite side of a case include:

- Conduct the interview in a private room that is free from distraction.
- Interview only one person at a time.
- Use short questions rather than complex compound questions.
- Avoid yes-or-no questions in favor of open-ended questions (which tend to elicit more information).
- Give the interviewee ample time to answer questions and ask him or her to expound on incomplete answers.
- Establish the factual basis for the interviewee's answers if it is not clear (i.e., how does the interviewee know that?).
- Keep the interview on track and do not let the interviewee talk at length about unrelated things.
- Do not reveal information to the interviewee, such as opinions that the expert intends to express.
- Maintain control of the interview while still being pleasant and cooperative.

Chapter 8

Historical Spending and Budgeting

As discussed in Chapter 2, the standard of living enjoyed by the spouses during a marriage is often one of the main factors in awarding spousal support and child support. One cannot determine the "reasonable need" of a spouse unless the actual expenses during the marriage are analyzed. The standard of living will be determined on the basis of historical expenditures, with some modifications or adjustments depending on local rules and/or the circumstances of the case.

It is important to know how your jurisdiction defines "during the marriage." In some locales, this could include the time up to the date of divorce, whereas it only includes the period up to the separation in other places.

Detailing Expenditures

In Chapter 6, we discussed how bank, brokerage, and credit card statements can be used in divorce cases to quantify and evaluate expenditures. Chapter 7 discussed the analysis and tabulation of expenditures. Here we take the process a step further and see how the detail and summary records may look as the forensic accountant is working with them.

As discussed previously, there is no standard for the period of time that should be analyzed to determine the standard of living during the marriage. Often the analysis of expenditures will be for a period of one to five years, with a preference toward the middle to upper end of the range. The key in selecting a period is determining whether it represents the spending during the recent years of marriage. The shorter the period analyzed, the more likely there will be unusual items of income or expense that may skew the results. However, analyzing a longer period increases the cost of the analysis and in some cases may be unnecessary.

A sample of a detailed transaction listing, with individual transactions logged and categorized, follows.

Bank	Acct #	Date	Year	Check #	Payee	Category	Deposits/ Payments	Checks/ Charges
Chase	3234	08/21/18	2018	1476	Carsons	Credit Card Payment		500.00
Chase	3234	08/22/18	2018	1477	Deposit	Deposit: Payroll	6,255.12	
Chase	3234	08/29/18	2018	1479	Animal Trackers	Repairs & Maintenance		135.00
Chase	3234	08/30/18	2018	1480	Orkin	Repairs & Maintenance		140.00
Chase	3234	09/04/18	2018	1481	Comenity	Credit Card Payment		500.00
Chase	3234	09/05/18	2018	1483	State Farm	Insurance		308.56
Chase	3234	08/06/18	2018	6611	University Club	Club Membership		300.00
Chase	3234	08/06/18	2018		Home Depot	Repairs & Maintenance	14.36	
Chase	3234	08/06/18	2018		Jewel	Groceries		56.12
Chase	3234	08/06/18	2018		The Barber Shop	Grooming		45.00
Chase	3234	08/06/18	2018		Jewel	Groceries		99.28
Chase	9601	02/05/18	2018		Blind & Drapery Store	Furnishings		1,190.00
Chase	9601	02/09/18	2018		Banner Plumbing Supply	Renovations		4,208.76
Chase	9601	02/17/18	2018		Northwest Electrical	Renovations		364.10
Chase	9601	03/01/18	2018		Annual Membership Fee	Bank Fees		95.00
Chase	9601	03/01/18	2018		Interest Charge	Interest Expense		119.62
Chase	9601	03/15/18	2018		Payment	Credit Card Payment	15,116.57	
Chase	9601	04/08/18	2018		AT&T	Telephone		175.00
Chase	9601	05/08/18	2018		Trugreen	Lawn/Snow		493.62

Expenditures could be classified in hundreds of different ways. It is best to narrow down the categories, however. The financial expert must break the categories down far enough that the summed data is meaningful, but not so far that the number of categories is overwhelming. The categories used will be based on personal preference and the financial affidavit form used in the jurisdiction, but a sample list of categories follows.

Activities	Garbage Removal	Pet Care
Auto: Fuel	Gifts	Pharmacy
Auto: Parking	Groceries	Shipping & Storage
Auto: Purchase	Grooming	Professional Fees
Auto: Service	Homeowners Association	Rent
Bank Fees	Household	Renovations
Cable/Internet	Insurance: Auto	Repairs & Maintenance
Cash Withdrawal	Insurance: Health	Taxes: Income
Charity	Insurance: Home	Taxes: Real Estate
Childcare	Insurance: Life	Taxi
Cleaning Service	Interest Expense	Telephone
Clothing	Interest Income	Transfer
Computer	Investments	Travel: Airfare
Credit Card Payment	Jewelry	Travel: Lodging
Deposit	Landscaping	Travel: Transportation
Dining	Medical: Doctor	Unknown
Electronics	Medical: Dental	Utilities
Entertainment	Miscellaneous	Wire In
Furnishings	Office Supplies	Wire Out

Categories are often straightforward and obvious. An Internet search can be done to identify payees, and the detail from the credit card statements (such as a telephone number of a retailer) may help determine what the expenditure was. For example, grocery stores, clothing stores, and restaurants are easily identifiable. Hotels and airlines can be quickly identified. Insurance companies are easy to ascertain, as are professional service firms like attorneys and accountants.

The individual items must be categorized based on their true substance. This might not be obvious in all cases, especially in situations involving loans, gifts, bartering, or payments to third parties who may not have directly provided goods or services. A category such as "unknown" can be a handy way to track items that do not immediately fit into an obvious category. The spouses will need to be consulted to categorize those items.

This process of categorizing transactions usually is not technically difficult. Instead, the difficulty lies in categorizing a large volume of transactions and in being consistent with the categories. It is important that two payments to the same party be placed in the same category, unless there is an unusual situation in which the two expenditures were for different purposes. If the expert is not consistent in categorizing expenses, it will cause problems later in the analysis.

Categorizing expenses is typically not done with accounting rules in mind. This is not an accounting exercise, and the purpose is not to prepare financial statements that follow typical accounting rules. Instead, it is an exercise in categorizing expenditures for a specific period of time for the specific purpose of the family law case. The categorization should be simple, straightforward, and useful to the litigation.

The financial expert should apply professional skepticism when using categories supplied by the spouses. It is possible that the spouses are not being truthful about the categories (e.g., a spouse may categorize charges for pornography under dining in an effort to disguise them) or may simply be mistaken. It is important to double-check categories identified by the spouses to the extent that it is possible and practical.

Key elements involved in properly classifying expenditures include:

- Classify expenditures correctly—Research payees and work with the client to determine the correct categories. Ensure the accuracy of the categories, especially if multiple staff members are working with the data.
- Classify expenditures consistently—Ensure that all expenditures with a given payee are categorized in the same way. If payments to a particular party can be classified in more than one way, document the distinction, and carefully review classifications. Again, with multiple staff members working with the data, it will be important to carefully evaluate the consistency of the categories.

- Split expenditures if necessary—A single payment may need to be split between two or more categories. Split the transaction accordingly, and document the basis for the split.
- Double-check categories—Look for items that are not classified correctly or consistently. This involves looking at a category in total and at the detail behind that total.
- Be prepared to explain classifications—The financial expert may be called upon to explain the categories and classifications in a written report or during testimony, so it is important to document how it was done. This is especially important if assumptions were used when assigning categories.

When the sides dispute the categorization of expenses, the expert witness should be cross-examined accordingly. It may be possible to point out to the court that the expert and his or her staff did not properly categorize items or were not consistent in their categorization.

Analyzing the Totals

The categorized figures should be summarized by month, quarter, or year. The specific case and its issues will dictate which period or periods should be evaluated. Often a monthly average will be calculated, either for the entire period under analysis or for multiple periods, such as each year.

The financial expert should review the totals with the following questions in mind:

- **Are the figures reasonable?** Did monthly expenses recur each month as expected, or was a month or two missed? Do the totals seem reasonable, or are they much higher or lower than expected? Have any expenses been double-counted? Were line items categorized correctly?
- **What are the details behind the totals?** Detailed transactions grouped by category should be scanned to look for anything unusual or questionable. Were payees categorized consistently? If not, was there a specific basis for the varying classifications?

- **Are there any categories that must be investigated further?** For example, large expenditures that appear to be related to an extramarital affair may need to be examined in detail. Items that may be related to a spouse's employment or business venture may need to be evaluated carefully.
- **What do the historical figures suggest about future income and expenses?** The historical figures may form a substantial basis for predicting future income and expenses. Do any of the historical expenses appear to be nonrecurring, so they should be excluded from projections?
- **Do the totals tend to support or refute claims made by either spouse about income or expenses?** Investigate substantial differences between estimates made by the spouses and the actual figures. Was the spouse incorrect? Is the analysis inaccurate? Are there other accounts that may have been excluded from the analysis in error? Are there other explanations for the differences?

Future income and expenses should be projected if the accounting expert is directed to do so. The expert must remember to consider how the figures might change over the years based on a number of factors. Consider whether cost of living increases or changing circumstances (e.g., children coming of age and moving out of the family residence) will affect the numbers.

Excluding Items from Marital Lifestyle

As discussed in Chapter 2, a number of different factors can influence the calculation of the standard of living or the marital lifestyle. On one end of the spectrum, a case can be made for including every single expense that was incurred during the marriage. However lavish the lifestyle during the marriage, a case can be made that an equivalent lifestyle should be funded after the divorce.

On the other end of the spectrum, some argue that only the necessities should be included in the marital lifestyle. Attorneys and experts might suggest that the lifestyle should include only basic expenses and exclude any sort of elective spending or luxuries. Of course, there is plenty of gray area in between, and it is rare that either of the extremes will provide a reasonable view of the true lifestyle of the parties.

Some of the more common items that could reasonably be argued for exclusion from the standard of living include:

- Funds for the extended family—Sometimes the spouses choose to provide support or gifts to extended family members. While this may have been a significant, ongoing expense, a case can be made that the extended family is not entitled to be supported or enriched from marital funds. Therefore, it may be reasonable to exclude those expenditures from the marital lifestyle and not consider them in any calculations related to support or asset division when divorcing.

- Vacations—Expenses for family and individual vacations can be an area of contention, especially if the family traveled extensively. When children are involved, it may get even more complicated. For example, a spouse who participated in four family vacations per year may claim that he or she is entitled to take four vacations with the children per year. If both parents did this, the children would have eight vacations per year, and the expenses would be substantially higher than during the marriage. An argument can be made that post-divorce expenses for leisure travel must stay within the family's total budget during the marriage, regardless of the frequency of travel. There may be several ways to analyze the travel expenditures and come up with a "vacation lifestyle" that is fair after separation.

- Excessive or unreasonable spending—As discussed in Chapter 2, an argument can be made that certain spending was unreasonable or excessive and, therefore, should be excluded from the lifestyle. This concept may be influenced by whether the spouse agreed to the excessive spending, either explicitly or implicitly.

- Nonmarital expenditures—It could be argued that expenses incurred without the knowledge or approval of the spouse should be considered nonmarital. This would especially be true of the expenditures related to illegal, dishonest, fraudulent, or immoral behavior. Things such as gambling, pornography, and drugs are often under this umbrella. If the spending provided no benefit to the family, it might be properly excluded from the standard of living.

- Nonrecurring expenditures—Certain expenditures will not recur due to the dissolution of the marriage. This may include expenses related to the wedding, anniversary parties, and other anniversary celebrations or vacations.

This list is not all-inclusive. Other items might also be excluded from the calculated marital lifestyle. It is important to have a firm basis for excluding items from the calculation so as to maintain the credibility of the financial expert and his or her calculations.

Preparing the Post-Divorce Budget

The results of the detailed analysis of expenditures may be used to prepare a post-divorce budget for one or both of the spouses. States have their own accepted formats and categories to be used when preparing the budget. There are a number of different ways to figure the spouse's post-divorce budget:

- Based on historical expenditures—This assumes that the spouse is entitled to live a lifestyle very similar to the lifestyle enjoyed during the marriage.
- Based on the current reality—The expenditures may be lower or higher after separation. For example, a spouse whose access to funds may be severely restricted may have much lower expenditures currently than during the marriage.
- Based on some combination of historical expenditures and current reality—The parties often disagree as to what spending is reasonable. If spending during the marriage was deemed excessive, should the spouses be able to continue excessive spending after the divorce? Or must the spouses reduce their spending to "reasonable" levels?

The most influential component of the post-divorce budget will likely be the standard of living during the marriage, which is discussed at length in Chapter 2. Local rules will impact how the standard of living or reasonable needs are calculated and, therefore, how the post-divorce budget should be assembled.

Insufficient Income or Assets

Many times, the standard of living enjoyed during the marriage cannot be replicated for both spouses after the marriage ends. A finite amount of money is available to the spouses, but certain expenses (such as housing) must now be paid twice (once for each spouse). Collectively the spouses may not be able to afford a residence for each that is equivalent to the one lived in during the marriage. Both spouses will likely have to limit their spending after the divorce in this case.

Also, supporting a similar lifestyle may require one spouse to deplete his or her assets after the divorce, whereas the other spouse may actually see his or her assets increase in value after the divorce. This type of situation must be taken into account during the property division and when arguing for support.

Chapter 9

Hidden Income

Finding hidden sources of income is important as it relates to spousal support. However, the discovery of income streams can also influence the division of assets. If one spouse has a larger income stream than previously disclosed, that spouse may not need as large a share of the assets divided during divorce. Clearly, the discovery of hidden income can significantly impact the financial outcome of a divorce or child support action.

Support calculations and asset divisions are fairly straightforward when spouses only have wage income from jobs at companies that are unrelated to the spouses. The income is verified with a W-2 or income tax return, and there is nothing complicated about the calculations.

The calculations are more complex when a spouse is self-employed, has an unusually close personal relationship with the employer, works in a position with nonwage compensation such as stock options, owns income-producing real estate, owns multiple businesses, or receives income from trusts or other entities. In these more complicated situations, a search for hidden sources of income should almost always be done.

Methods to Hide Income

Some of the most common methods of hiding income on a personal level are discussed next. In Chapter 12, we discuss how a spouse may hide business revenue.

Underreport Income on Income Tax Returns

Since income tax returns are a common starting point for analyzing income available for support, income may be intentionally underreported on the tax return. The government has certain procedures in place to prevent underreporting of income, but business owners and investors have ample opportunity to lie about their income. It is common in a family law matter to accept the tax returns as the truth, but in certain cases this is a dangerous tactic. In cases in which one spouse knows there was manipulation of figures, it is especially important to validate the numbers.

Use Offshore Accounts

Offshore bank and investment accounts are used by spouses to hide both assets (the account balance) and income (the money coming into the account on a recurring basis). It may be difficult to find overseas accounts, particularly if the accounts are opened in a country known for banking secrecy. If the accounts are found, the even bigger hurdle is finding a way to seize funds belonging to the marital estate. Hiding money overseas is attractive because of the difficulty in locating and acquiring the funds, both because it takes so much time and effort and because there may be a great cost in doing so.

Withhold Pay and Benefits

If a spouse is an owner or executive of a closely held business, it may be easy for him or her to have pay and benefits withheld during the pendency of a family law case. A lower-level employee may also have success with such a tactic if he or she has a close enough relationship with owners or executives of an employer. There could be a verbal agreement in place to reimburse the owner, executive, or employee for the withheld pay and benefits once the divorce or child support action is closed. This is one of the reasons why it is so important to carefully evaluate earnings after a divorce is finalized.

Get Paid in Cash

Income may be hidden when a spouse is paid in cash for services provided to employers or other parties. "Cash under the table" is a common method used to hide an employer-employee relationship and shield the income from the taxing authorities or other parties. If there is a known history of cash payments, it may be an easier issue to evaluate because historical payments could be used as a basis to estimate current and future cash receipts. If there is no known history, there may only be suspicions of such payments, and finding proof may be difficult.

Receive Perks and Benefits

Employers often offer their employees perks and benefits such as expense accounts, automobiles, meal allowances, and medical reimbursement. The value of these perks can easily total thousands of dollars a year or more. It may be difficult to uncover the existence of these items, especially if the employer does not report them for tax purposes. Do not assume that the employer is following the tax laws and reporting all compensation, as many companies inadvertently or purposely fail to report items that are taxable to the employee.

Barter

Individuals and businesses can trade goods or services, referred to as barter transactions, and fail to report income related to the products or services received in the exchange. Revenue and net income are usually both under-stated as a result of barter transactions, and such income is difficult to find because there is often no paper trail associated with the transactions. Although tax laws require reporting of barter income, those laws are often ignored.

Fail to Disclose a Business Venture

When cases involve closely held businesses, investment income, rental properties, or other business activities, there is a risk that a spouse will not fully disclose all of the ventures. The risk is even greater if the spouse has a history of creating multiple business entities. It is nearly impossible to keep up with all of the businesses. In a contentious divorce, the spouse may turn to new entities and ventures to hide income.

One concern is businesses that are completely unknown to the spouse. This may take the work of a qualified private investigator to uncover. The other concern may be a new venture related to one already in existence.

Income from a known business entity can be quietly transferred to a new entity, and the business owner can simply say that the original business lost some customers.

Run Income Through a Hidden Entity

It is not uncommon for an individual to form a trust or other type of entity to conceal income. The hidden entity receives the income in the form of cash or other valuable assets and holds that income until such time as the family law case concludes or the individual determines that the assets can be withdrawn without fear of discovery.

Methods to Uncover Hidden Income

In general, hidden income is often found because of the carelessness of the spouse. No matter how hard he or she may try to hide evidence of certain transactions, clues are often left behind. Scrutiny of income tax returns can sometimes reveal evidence of assets or sources of income that were previously unknown or undisclosed.

A detailed analysis of bank, brokerage, and credit card accounts will often provide evidence of sources of income as well. Large checks made out to cash, significant cash withdrawals, substantial payments to unknown entities, and transfers to previously undisclosed accounts are warning signs of hidden assets. Large cash transactions must be explained, and absent proof of an asset purchase, it is possible that the cash was hidden or used for nonmarital purposes. The primary concern as it relates to hidden income is that the cash was used to purchase an investment or real estate, either of which could produce income for the spouse.

A relatively small, insignificant transaction through a bank, brokerage, or credit card account may be all that is needed to raise suspicions and point the financial expert toward a source of income. Thus, the detailed analysis of expenditures discussed in Chapter 8 can be used not only to determine the standard of living during the marriage but also to look for hidden sources of income.

One method of obtaining financial information that is often overlooked is through source documents seized immediately prior to the filing of divorce. A spouse may have legitimate access to cash receipts, canceled checks, money order receipts, and other receipts that may evidence income or expenses. These types of items can be sorted, tabulated, and analyzed to draw conclusions about income. Although the "second set of books" is often alluded to in a joking way, the existence of a second set of records is actually a common occurrence. Savvy businesspeople like to track the real profitability of business operations, even when deliberately underreporting income for tax or divorce purposes. Obtaining that set of records can be invaluable to the family law case.

Underreported Income on Income Tax Returns

It is difficult to discover underreported income on an income tax return without some insider knowledge. The Internal Revenue Service has procedures in place to force individuals to fully report income from employment, investments, and the like, so the risk of missing income from one of these is lower. The most likely discovery of underreported income will be related to a business venture, such as a corporation or rental property, but identifying the income may be difficult to do with only income tax returns. See Chapter 12 for a detailed discussion of uncovering hidden income in business ventures.

Offshore Accounts

Offshore bank and investment accounts are most likely to be discovered by analyzing known bank accounts. The spouse hiding the overseas accounts may be careless and use a known account to fund the hidden account. Another likely scenario is that the owner of the foreign account may leave behind evidence of a relationship with the country in which the account was opened, such as correspondence or other documents.

There is no master database that tracks bank and investment accounts and their owners. Any investigator who says they can find bank accounts using databases and other resources is most likely accessing information illegally. This is a dangerous way to proceed in a family law case and could end up damaging the credibility of the client who hires such an investigator.

Withheld Pay and Benefits

It is difficult to obtain evidence of withheld pay and benefits. One way to approach this situation is to analyze past earnings and make a case that the current reported earnings do not reflect the current effort. The financial expert may look for unusual decreases in benefits. Explanations should be sought for the decreases in pay and benefits, and these explanations should be verified to the extent possible.

The financial expert may gather circumstantial evidence that shows the business is as prosperous as ever, so the reduction in pay and benefits is phony. The other approach may be to closely monitor pay and benefits after the divorce is finalized. If the expert can analyze earnings after the divorce, there may be evidence that the company distributed the withheld pay.

Cash Payments

Cash payments are an attractive way to conceal income because they leave no paper trail. The most likely way cash income will be uncovered is by analyzing expenditures. If the known expenditures documented via bank, brokerage, and credit card accounts are obviously insufficient compared to the known lifestyle of the spouse, it can be inferred that the spouse is being paid in cash and using that cash to fund part of the lifestyle.

If there is a history of cash compensation and the spouse has direct knowledge of that, it may be helpful in the case to give context to the issue. For example, if the spouse knows that a company has been paying the other party cash for services for the last ten years, it may be inferred that the cash compensation has continued. However, the court may be interested in seeing other evidence that supports the contention that cash compensation is currently being received.

Receipt of Perks and Benefits

Perks and benefits can be uncovered by subpoenaing the records of the employer. Some of the items will be shown on the employee's W-2, but others will not. Force the employer to disclose each of the benefits the employee is receiving and the value of those benefits. It may be necessary to ask very specific questions about the perks. Refer to the "Other Fringe Benefits" section in Chapter 11 for a list of potential perks.

In the case of a self-employed individual, the perks and benefits will likely only be uncovered through a detailed analysis of accounting records. The books and records may show the company has paid for items that are of a personal nature for the benefit of the owner or executive. It may be difficult to prove whether meals and travel are business-related or personal, but these expenses are often suspect.

Barter

Hidden barter transactions are difficult to uncover because no paper trail is generally left behind. The most likely way to discover barter transactions done by businesses is through the sudden disappearance of a long-time customer or vendor. It is possible that business is being done off-books to avoid documenting the transactions. On a personal level, barter income will likely be discovered only if the individual is found to be in possession of valuable goods for which no evidence of purchase can be established.

Failure to Disclose a Business Venture

An undisclosed business venture can be discovered with techniques discussed in Chapter 12.

Hidden Entities

Secret entities are difficult to uncover, especially if the spouse has undocumented ties to the entity. A beneficiary of a trust usually receives a K-1 for tax-reporting purposes, so that relationship is easy to discover. However, if the spouse does not have a documented relationship to the entity (e.g., is not named as the beneficiary of a trust), it may be next to impossible to discover.

It may be necessary to hire a private investigator who is skilled at uncovering personal and business relationships to have a chance at finding these hidden entities. However, the target may evade discovery if he or she is adept at hiding the details of relationships.

Other Complicated Income Sources

Income Disguised as Expenses

Closely held businesses can create a lot of controversy in divorce. The party who is involved in the business may utilize business funds to pay personal expenses and record those expenditures as business expenses. This makes the business look less profitable, so the owner's reported income is lower. At the same time, the owner has fewer personal expenses to be paid out of personal funds, so the cost of his or her lifestyle appears lower.

Some common personal expenses that may be recorded improperly as business expenses follow:

- Travel and entertainment
- Rent
- Automobile lease or loan payment
- Wages to phantom employees—For example, the business owner may pay wages to a friend or family member who is not really performing services for the company.
- Telephone
- Petty cash withdrawals
- School tuition and expenses
- Legal fees
- Social club dues and usage costs

The payment of personal expenses by the business should be recorded as compensation to the party receiving the benefit. This causes the net income of the business to be properly reported and recognizes that the party is indeed receiving compensation.

Undistributed Income

Partnerships and corporations (both C corporations and S corporations) owned by divorcing spouses may have earnings that are not distributed to the owners. The failure to distribute income may be for a legitimate business purpose, such as funding expansions or capital projects. Alternatively, the owners may choose to withhold funds that could be distributed to the owners in an attempt to manipulate their personal income or cash flow. Some business owners will argue that even though a business was profitable on paper, the fact that no money was distributed means those profits should not be counted as income.

Undistributed income should be included in income calculations for the owner. The owner has control over whether the income is distributed and can easily manipulate things to his or her benefit when divorcing. The choice to take or not take a distribution does not change the fact that the income was earned and the owner of the company has a legal right to it.

A business owner may also choose to stop taking a paycheck when family law proceedings are ongoing. It may be necessary to determine what reasonable compensation for the owner should be, based on his or her knowledge and skills, involvement in the business, hours worked, duties performed, contributions to the operations, and market value of the services.

Finding Hidden Income Example

A business owner sometimes hides income "in plain sight." In other words, he or she may not commit any of the overt acts discussed in this chapter. Rather, he or she has sources of income that are readily ascertainable if a forensic accountant with the appropriate expertise is retained.

Edward was trying to avoid his full support obligations by underreporting his income to the court. He owned a business that provided equipment repair services in a specialized industry. The niche services were provided on an emergency basis and were therefore very lucrative. The company leased a commercial building from Edward, where they manufactured custom parts used in the repairs. Edward also owned two rental homes.

In filings with the court, Edward disclosed his wages from the company, rental income, and interest and dividends. In total, he disclosed income of $480,000 per year. A detailed analysis of the personal and business income tax returns, financial statements, general ledgers for the business and rental properties, bank statements, and credit card statements was done to determine if there were other sources of income.

The wages were verified, but the rental income and interest and dividends were underreported. Edward ignored the income of the service company, since it was a C corporation and he had not distributed dividends to himself. Although the income had not yet been distributed, Edward was the only shareholder of the corporation and he had complete control over whether or not the earnings were distributed. Therefore, it was fair to include the company's earnings in his personal income.

The analysis of the bank statements and credit card statements in conjunction with the general ledgers of the service company and the rental business revealed substantial personal expenses paid on Edward's behalf. These included personal luxury vehicles, fuel for personal vehicles, housekeepers, boat expenses, jewelry, and personal travel. It was also noted that there were likely a number of personal items that could not be readily identified from the statements and any such items would increase the calculated income.

The figures disclosed by Edward versus the numbers calculated by the forensic accountant were as follows:

	Disclosed	Actual
Wages	$180,000	$ 180,000
Interest & Dividends	3,000	24,000
Business Income	0	570,000
Personal Expenses	0	62,000
Rental Income	297,000	318,000
Total Annual	**$480,000**	**$1,154,000**

The total income calculated by the forensic accountant was more than double the amount Edward disclosed. The undisclosed or hidden income was $674,000 per year, and it was likely that there was even more income that had not been discovered. None of the income was hidden in a traditional way, but it was undisclosed by Edward in the hope that it would never be uncovered. It was only through a detailed analysis of a significant number of financial documents that the truth was revealed.

Proof of Income via Expenditures

In some cases, it is nearly impossible to determine income from the documents provided. This is often the case for self-employed individuals or those employed in nontraditional capacities. A self-employed person may manipulate the earnings of the business, use the business as a personal piggybank, or obscure his or her earnings. The party may not provide documentation sufficient to determine his or her earnings, may provide documents that do not appear authentic, or may purposely provide confusing or contradictory financial information. This makes it extremely difficult to determine the true earnings of the spouse.

When income cannot be determined based on the documents provided by a spouse, the expenditures method of calculating income may be necessary. The forensic accountant analyzes the spouse's spending to substantiate his or her income. It is not unusual for a spouse to claim he or she is earning little to nothing from the business while spending lavishly on houses, trips, automobiles, and other luxury purchases.

Spending is analyzed, and a calculation is done to determine the income required to support the level of spending by the spouse. This analysis does not provide direct proof of the spouse's income. Instead, the forensic accountant uses circumstantial evidence to infer the amount of income that is necessary to live the spouse's lifestyle.

Methodology

Expenditures are analyzed and categorized as described in Chapter 8. An additional step may be added to the process if it is suspected that the spouse has undocumented spending (which could be evidence of concealed income). Information on this spending may come from insiders with information on vacations taken, vehicles purchased, or other costly business or recreational interests.

Everyday spending done without a paper trail should be considered as well. If the spouse is suspected of using concealed cash income for daily expenditures such as gasoline, groceries, dining out, and household supplies, the financial expert should examine the documented spending for those categories. Is the documented spending reasonable based on what is known about the spouse's lifestyle?

If the documented spending appears insufficient compared to the spouse's known lifestyle, then additional expenditures should be estimated. For example, to estimate the spending on gasoline, the financial expert should take into account the spouse's commute to work, the number of car drivers in the household, and personal activities that require driving. From these items, mileage can be estimated, and using historical prices of gasoline, an estimate of spending can be developed.

The financial expert can use known facts and common-sense assumptions to make reasonable estimates for many categories of spending. Consider the following examples:

- The mortgage payment can be calculated based on the purchase price of the home and details of the mortgage.
- Real estate taxes can be determined through public records.
- A car payment can be estimated based on information regarding the purchase price of the car and typical financing rates.

Expenditures for food and clothing can be estimated using sources such as the national standards for allowable living expenses published by the Internal Revenue Service. A recent example is included in Appendix C.

In general, estimates of spending can be calculated using publicly available information. There are not specific accounting rules to be applied to these calculations. However, the key to creating reliable estimates is being conservative and using supportable assumptions. Opposing counsel will readily attack radical assumptions or unsupported figures.

The expert adds the documented expenses and estimated expenses and determines the amount of income required to fund them. This amount is compared to reported income; the difference between reported income and the income required to fund the expenditures might represent unreported income.

Expenditures Method Example

Brian Williams owned partial interests in nine entities invested in income-producing real estate. His personal income tax returns, as well as the income tax returns of the business entities, generally showed losses for the last five years. However, one of the entities (a sole proprietorship owned by Brian) averaged net income of about $500,000 per year.

During the divorce, his spouse Amanda Williams disclosed that the family always had a high standard of living, and Brian maintained that standard of living since he filed for divorce. She stated that the business entities distributed cash to Brian regularly, which is how the family's lifestyle was funded.

Brian contended that he had *no income* from these entities (his only potential source of income from employment or personal services), as evidenced by the income tax returns. He claimed that he did not receive the net income from the sole proprietorship. Instead, Brian said the earnings of that entity were reinvested in his other business ventures.

Brian received quarterly or annual distributions from some of the entities, but the extent of the distributions could not be fully investigated because Brian produced only partial information and documentation. It was unclear if his failure to produce the documents (despite multiple requests) was intentional.

The forensic accountant completed an analysis of Brian's expenditures from his bank and credit card accounts for 2019 and summarized the figures shown here:

2019 Expenditures Summary

	BOA 4711	Chase 7643	Chase 0217	Chase 9237	TOTAL
Jan	5,722	6,684	844	38,199	51,449
Feb	3,105	3,079	1,644	15,252	23,080
Mar	4,304	3,345	356	41,194	49,199
Apr	2,218	3,471	1,943	39,889	47,521
May	5,601	4,322	812	32,103	42,838
Jun	3,498	5,345	363	23,516	32,722
Jul	1,257	1,649	242	31,054	34,202

2019 Expenditures Summary *(continued)*

	BOA 4711	Chase 7643	Chase 0217	Chase 9237	TOTAL
Aug	6,733	7,712	534	16,977	31,956
Sep	2,484	3,129	1,208	18,377	25,198
Oct	4,388	4,360	946	36,034	45,728
Nov	3,345	2,817	566	40,284	47,012
Dec	6,124	3,189	523	20,411	30,247
Average					$39,516

On average, Brian spent over $39,000 each month on personal items. We multiply this figure by 12 to annualize the spending, which is over $474,000. This total excluded transfers of funds from Brian to his business entities. When confronted with these figures, Brian stated that he funded his personal expenditures with loans from the businesses to him.

An analysis of deposits to Brian's bank accounts showed three transactions during the year totaling $176,000 that could be loans from the businesses. However, the expenditures analysis showed that Brian paid $200,000 to those businesses during the year, negating the potential loans received.

The financial expert therefore determined that Brian's lifestyle of almost $39,000 per month was not funded with loans but instead must have been funded with income from the business entities. Additionally, it was noted that the estimated $474,000 in annual personal expenditures could have been funded with the $500,000 of average annual net income produced by the sole proprietorship.

Note that this example is simplified for the purpose of presenting it here. However, it gives the reader a flavor for how an expenditures analysis can be used and presented to prove income.

Other Sources of Funds

A primary argument against using the expenditures method to prove income is that the spending may be funded from a source other than income. It is therefore important for the financial expert to consider other sources of funding for the personal expenses, such as:

- Loans
- Gifts or inheritances
- Sales of assets
- Advances from business interests
- Cash hoards

The forensic accountant should attempt to identify or rule out these sources of funds before opining on the income necessary to support the lifestyle. The first four items on the list are verifiable. For example, if the spouse sold assets, there will be paperwork related to the transaction and a paper trail of the funds.

A spouse may claim that the excess expenditures were funded via a cash hoard that was being depleted. It is difficult to prove whether a cash hoard existed, particularly since cash hoards are often kept because they are so difficult to trace or track. The financial expert should push for proof of a cash hoard from the spouse claiming it existed and was used to fund expenditures. The spouse should be asked the following questions about the alleged cash hoard:

- How did the money get accumulated?
- When was it accumulated?
- Where was it kept?
- Why was it not disclosed until now?

By delving into these questions, it may be possible to prove that the cash hoard is fictitious.

It may be possible to use circumstantial evidence to disprove the existence of a cash hoard. Analyzing income and expenses for periods during the time the hoarding allegedly occurred may prove that there was no cash available to hide. Evidence of financial difficulties during the period of alleged hoarding may tend to disprove the existence of the hoard, as a person with financial problems would be unlikely to keep a stash of cash untouched. This would be especially true if, during the time of financial problems, personal possessions were being liquidated, payments on debt were being missed, credit cards were being pushed to their limits, or substantial interest was accruing on credit lines.

Basis for the Analysis

The primary argument usually made by opposing counsel against a lifestyle analysis done via the expenditures method is that it relies on circumstantial evidence to prove income. The family lawyer would much rather the court base support and asset division decisions on documented sources of income. Therein lies the whole purpose of this lifestyle analysis: It identified red flags that strongly suggested that the spouse had *undocumented and undisclosed* sources of income.

Although the evidence may be circumstantial, a strong case can be made for using the lifestyle analysis if the expert is experienced enough and can present the results properly. If the spouse contends that the source of funds was something other than hidden income, the spouse should be bound to prove that assertion. If the funds allegedly came from borrowing or gifts, the historical receipt of loans or gifts could easily be substantiated with documents produced by the spouse. In the absence of such proof, the explanations remain unsubstantiated and therefore suspect.

Difficulties related to the circumstantial nature of the evidence should not deter a litigant from doing a lifestyle analysis. The calculation is done when there are suspicions or allegations of undocumented or unreported sources of funds and/or to document the parties' standard of living over time. It is only natural that there may be some unanswered questions or imprecisions in the calculation.

However, when done properly, the expenditures method can be an effective method of proving income. It can be particularly effective when paired with other evidence that tends to support the calculated level of income.

Chapter 10

Hidden Assets

Hidden assets can impact both the property division and the award of support payments. Assets hidden by one spouse deprive the other spouse of his or her share. If the hidden assets include income-producing assets such as a business venture or an investment portfolio, the spouse receiving support could receive a lesser amount of support to which he or she is entitled.

Some of the most common personal and business assets hidden during a family law case include:

- Offshore bank accounts—Bank accounts can be hidden no matter where they are established. Overseas bank accounts are often easier to hide and more difficult for a spouse to access even if they are discovered.
- Real estate—Rental real estate (income-producing) is easier to find because it often creates tax paperwork. Real estate that is not rented may not create a tax paper trail, making it harder to find.
- Collectibles, including antiques, jewelry, precious gems, coins, sports memorabilia, and artwork—These types of personal property are portable and, therefore, easy to move and hide.
- Rare livestock, including animals such as thoroughbred horses—Even though these assets are a bit more difficult to hide because of their size and the care required, their true value might be concealed.
- Assets transferred or sold to related parties and entities—Friends, family, and business associates may take possession of valuable assets while

a divorce is pending. Cash, business interests, investments, stocks, and bonds are some of the more common items that may be given to related parties for safekeeping during the family law case.

Spouses should make comprehensive lists of all assets they believe are owned at the time of separation. Making those lists early is critical so that the forensic accountant has time to investigate the status of each asset.

Identifying and Classifying Assets

The first step in determining whether any assets have been hidden is identifying and properly classifying the known assets. Identification of assets can be problematic, particularly with high-net-worth clients who own many assets and entities. Immediately upon separation (or in preparation for separation), the spouses should begin compiling lists of known assets and liabilities. The following assets should be included in the inventory:

- Bank accounts
- Investment and brokerage accounts
- Stocks not in investment or brokerage accounts
- Real estate
- Vehicles
- Aircraft
- Boats
- Jewelry
- Art
- Collections (coins, sports memorabilia, precious gems, antiques, etc.)
- Personal possessions including household furnishings
- Tools and equipment
- Whole life insurance policies

A listing of liabilities should include:

- Mortgages
- Personal loans

- Student loans
- Lines of credit
- Credit cards
- Amounts owed to any other creditor (medical, legal, utilities, etc.)

To the extent possible, account statements should be gathered and secured. Many spouses wait until discovery starts in earnest to begin gathering account statements. However, the longer they wait, the more difficult it may be to obtain the statements. Even though the statements can be subpoenaed directly from financial institutions, proactively gathering and copying statements or accessing data online may help ensure that all accounts and assets are accounted for. Also, the sooner the spouse has the statements, the more leverage he or she may have in the divorce. Having information sooner rather than later is always preferable.

The assets must be valued, and the date of valuation depends on local laws. Relevant dates for the valuation of assets may include:

- Date of marriage
- Date of receipt of a gift or inheritance
- Date of separation
- Date on which the divorce petition was filed
- Date of trial
- Date on which the divorce is granted
- An agreed-upon date

When assets are divided, the court may consider several important factors such as:

- Length of the marriage
- Age and health of the spouses
- Marital standard of living
- Contributions of each spouse to marital assets
- Separate property owned by each spouse
- Earning capacity of each spouse
- Tax consequences of the property division
- Custodial provisions for the children

Income, expenditures, and asset values end up being interrelated in the divorce. Discovering hidden assets or income can impact more than one portion of the divorce, multiplying the importance of that discovery.

Asset Search Client Questionnaire

Unknown assets often can only be discovered with a thorough search. If after identifying and classifying known assets the attorney or client still thinks assets are being concealed, it is good practice to go through the following questions with a client. Even though clients may know little about accounting or law, they know the subject of the asset investigation better than the retained professionals, and they can provide invaluable clues to help uncover assets.

This questionnaire was developed by Philip Segal of Charles Griffin Intelligence, LLC. Mr. Segal is an attorney who works exclusively as an investigator, doing due diligence and asset searches. He is an expert in complex international financial transactions and is dedicated to ethical fact-finding. He suggests asking clients the following questions to help guide the asset search:

1. What are all the names of the people to be searched?
   a. List any other names you know they have used. Single names? Other married names? Variations of their current names? Have they used their middle name or initials instead of their first name, for example?
   b. What about nicknames? Sometimes people named Robert Johnson can be known as "Steve" because of a middle name or for some other reason (they looked like a certain Steve in high school, for example).
2. When were they born?
3. Where were they born?
4. Are they (re)married?
   a. What is their spouse's name?
   b. Have they been married previously? If so, what were their prior spouses' names?
5. What are the names of their parents and siblings? Are they particularly close to parents and siblings, and if so, which ones?

6. Where do they live?
   a. What are the addresses?
   b. Do they own property there? Keep in mind this includes real estate, as well as cars, boats, planes, etc. And real estate is more than just homes: It also includes land and commercial buildings.
7. What phone numbers are associated with them? (Think about international numbers as well.)
   a. Home
   b. Office
   c. Mobiles
   d. Any phone number they used to have but no longer have
8. Where do they go on vacation? How frequently?
   a. Do they own property there?
   b. What are the addresses?
   c. What are the phone numbers for those properties?
9. Where do they bank? Include both personal and business banking relationships.
   a. Currently
   b. Previously
10. Do they have investments?
    a. Stocks? Bonds? Property? Other businesses?
    b. Do they have any paid insurance policies with cash value?
    c. Do they have any annuities that you know of?
    d. Do they have any retirement accounts?
11. Where do they currently work?
    a. What is the address there?
    b. What is their position?
12. Do they have any ownership interest where they work?
13. Do they have or have they had any partners?
    a. What are the full names of the partners?
    b. Where do they live?
    c. What are their addresses?
14. Have they had any previous jobs?
    a. What were the addresses and phone numbers there?
    b. What was their position?

15. Have they had any ownership interest where they previously worked?
16. Do they currently own any companies?
    a. What are the names of the companies?
    b. What do they do?
    c. What are their addresses?
    d. What phone numbers are associated with them?
17. Have they previously owned any companies?
    a. If so, what were the companies called?
    b. Are there any naming conventions they've relied on? For example, initials of names? City names? Variations on the same name? (St. Mark Co., St. Mark Associates, St. Mark Partnerships, or consecutive names like Alpha I, Alpha II, etc.)
    c. What did the companies do?
    d. What are/were their addresses?
    e. What phone numbers are/were associated with them?
18. If you were this person, where would you think the smartest place to hide assets would be?
19. Where would this person expect you to look for assets?
20. Look back over all your answers. Is there anything about this person that's missing that could possibly help us find assets?

Classifying Marital or Separate Property

After assets are identified, they must be classified as marital or separate property. If there is a dispute as to whether assets are actually separate, the party claiming separateness may need to prove that the assets (and the funds put into the assets) were kept separate. Tracing funds establishes the source of an asset, following the funds until they became the current form. This includes the acquisition, maintenance, and disposal of the asset and its proceeds.

When determining whether an asset is separate or marital property, important factors include:

- Ownership or acquisition prior to the marriage
- Inheritance
- Gift
- Award from personal injury
- Proceeds from sale of separate property invested into another asset
- Property acquired during the marriage with separate funds
- Property that is separate by agreement
- Rent, profit, income, dividends, or interest generated by an asset acquired prior to marriage

Assets that were once separate can become marital property through a number of different actions such as:

- Retitling property into the names of both spouses
- Commingling separate and marital funds, and being unable to trace assets to a separate property source
- Using proceeds from the sale of separate property to acquire a marital or community asset
- Using marital or community funds to maintain or pay the debt on separate property
- Gifting separate assets to the marital estate

A forensic accountant may need to trace assets, the funds used to acquire and maintain the assets, and the proceeds of the disposition of the assets. This is done in much the same way that income and expenditures are traced for a lifestyle analysis, but the tracing will be focused only on a particular asset or group of assets.

Tracing of funds can get complicated, particularly when trying to prove where specific funds went. Suppose a bank account has a balance of $10,000 and the account is one spouse's separate property. A deposit of $3,000 of marital funds is made. The account now has a balance of $13,000. A withdrawal of $2,000 is made from the account. Did the $2,000 come from the separate property or the marital property? It is impossible to know because the money is mixed together in the account.

A common assumption the financial expert may make is "first in, first out" (FIFO). He or she will assume that the funds that went into an account first are the funds that will go out of the account first. While that is a reasonable assumption to use, it must be acknowledged that this methodology does not change the fact that it is impossible to segregate or separately identify funds once they are deposited into a bank account.

Hiding Assets

The number of ways assets can be hidden when a divorce is pending is limited only by the imagination of the spouse doing the hiding. This section considers some of the more common ways that assets are hidden.

Hide Cash

Cash is an attractive asset to hide because it is so difficult to find, and therefore it may be a good way to deprive a spouse of a share of the asset. Often, cash is used because it lacks a paper trail; therefore, its existence and movement is sometimes impossible to prove. Cash could be hidden in a house, in a safe deposit box, or with trusted friends or relatives. No one may really know how much cash was accumulated, over what time it was accumulated, the source of the funds, or on what cash was previously spent. Accumulating a large sum of money will take a substantial amount of time and will risk coming under scrutiny in light of anti–money laundering rules.

Use Cash to Purchase Assets

Cash can be used to purchase valuable assets that may be hidden during divorce. Cash withdrawals or cash back from deposits into bank accounts should be considered red flags, as it will be difficult or impossible to prove how the cash was used. The cash, particularly large amounts, is at risk of being deposited into secret accounts or used to secretly purchase income-producing assets.

Open Secret Accounts

A party can open bank, brokerage, and credit accounts that are not disclosed to the spouse. This is especially effective if the accounts are opened with institutions with which the parties have no prior history. The spouse may have no idea that the accounts exist. Accounts opened overseas will be difficult to identify, and it will be even more difficult to access the funds in the account.

Purchase Overlooked or Undervalued Items

Large, obvious purchases such as automobiles or homes are front and center in a family law case. Works of art, expensive home furnishings, or cutting-edge electronics do not generate as much interest. These types of personal property can be overlooked, and their true value may be difficult to ascertain. Jewelry purchases may generate interest, and jewelry is very easy to hide because of its relatively small size. Loose gemstones are even easier to overlook or hide. Items such as tools or lawn care equipment are often ignored, even though the property has value to the marital estate.

Undervalue Assets

A spouse may purposely underreport the value of assets, hoping the true value is not discovered prior to the divorce becoming final. For example, jewelry or artwork is difficult to value without an appraisal. Even business entities, which are often subjected to business valuations during the divorce process, can manipulated by the owners to appear less valuable. (See Chapter 12 for more on the manipulation of business entities in divorce.)

Overpay Creditors

A creative spouse may overpay the taxing authorities or other creditors while a family law case is pending, hopeful that the refund of the overpayment does not arrive until the case is closed. A typical creditor in a scheme like this may be the Internal Revenue Service or a credit card company. The funds are shifted away from the marital estate so the other spouse cannot lay claim to them, with the refund fully benefitting the scheming spouse.

Understate Revenue

A closely held business can intentionally understate revenue, which helps the owner conceal assets. When customers pay their accounts, it is easy to divert the funds because the accounts are not in the financial statements.

Pay Down Loans Secured with Assets

A spouse may make extraordinary payments on a loan secured with assets such as real estate. This depletes cash while increasing the equity in the assets. The hope may be that the spouse will be unaware of the increase in equity and, therefore, may miss out on a share of the true value of the assets.

Establish Accounts in the Names of Others

Beware of a spouse putting assets in the name of a child, a girlfriend or boyfriend, a close friend, or a family member. This is a simple method used to hide funds, with relatively little chance of being discovered without a forensic analysis of the finances. If the funds are discovered, it is hoped that having someone else's name on the account may still keep the funds out of the marital estate.

Transfer Assets

A spouse may give or sell assets to a friend, relative, or other close associate while a divorce is pending. The alleged sale will typically be at less than fair market value so that the other spouse's half of the proceeds is artificially depressed. A sale at less than fair market value suggests the sale is a sham transaction that will be reversed once the family law case is closed.

Other Sham Transactions

Divorcing spouses may "loan" money to family or friends or "start a business" with someone. These transactions could be legitimate; however, many times they are not. When they are shams, the goal is transferring cash or valuable assets out of the marital estate.

Uncovering Hidden Assets

In general, the most common way hidden assets are discovered in a divorce case is through a detailed analysis of financial documents. Often the spouse hiding the assets leaves clues behind. No matter how careful the spouse may be, at least *some* evidence of the existence of the assets may remain. Thus, expenditures should be detailed as described in Chapter 8, and the financial expert should complete a careful analysis of suspicious transactions.

Like the search for hidden income, financial documents such as cash receipts, canceled checks, money order receipts, and other receipts may help uncover hidden assets. A search for the "second set of books" may yield valuable information that points to hidden assets.

Income Tax Returns

A personal income tax return can be an excellent starting point for identifying hidden assets. Certain income and expense items are reported to the Internal Revenue Service and, therefore, must be included on an individual's tax return. Income and expenses reported on a tax return should be traced back to the underlying assets.

Listed below are the items reported on a personal federal income tax return along with the related assets that may be indicated by the data on the tax returns. A sample of a 2017 personal income tax return (Form 1040), a 2018 personal income tax return, and Schedule 1 are included in Appendix A for reference.

- Interest—This income item may indicate the existence of bank accounts, certificates of deposit, bonds, investment accounts, or loans receivable.
- Dividends—The existence of bank accounts, investment accounts, stocks, or other investments in business entities may be indicated by dividends.

- IRA distributions, pensions, annuities—This income item points to the existence of retirement accounts, annuities, or other valuable retirement assets.
- Business income or loss—Income reported here signifies sole proprietorships, single-member LLCs, or other sources of income, such as royalties.
- Capital gain or loss—This may point to investment accounts, stocks, business interests, or other investments.
- Rental real estate, royalties, partnerships, S corporations, trusts—This indicates the existence of income-producing assets (real estate or business) or an interest in estates or trusts.
- Farm income—Reported farm income points to farming activities, including valuable assets such as real estate and livestock.
- Health savings account deduction—This deduction signifies the existence of a medical-related savings account.
- SEP, SIMPLE, qualified plans—This indicates the existence of retirement accounts for self-employed individuals.
- IRA deduction—An IRA deduction signifies the existence of retirement accounts.
- Foreign tax credit—This credit signifies investment accounts with foreign holdings or investments in foreign countries.
- Income tax withheld and estimated tax payments—These items should be evaluated to determine whether excessive amounts are being withheld or paid as a method of hiding assets.
- Penalty on early withdrawal of savings—The disposition of the withdrawn funds should be investigated.

The following items on Schedule A (also in Appendix A) may also indicate the existence of assets:

- General sales taxes—This item could point to the purchase of substantial assets.
- Real estate taxes—This item may indicate the existence of real estate.
- Personal property taxes—This item could point to the existence of an automobile.

- Home mortgage interest—This item may also indicate the existence of real estate.
- Investment interest paid—This item can indicate the existence of investment accounts.

Bank, Brokerage, and Credit Card Account Records

Like hidden income, hidden assets can be uncovered through a detailed analysis of transactions in known bank, brokerage, and credit card accounts. Large cash withdrawals, cashiers' checks, or transfers could be used to purchase hidden assets.

Expenditures funded by bank, brokerage, or credit card accounts may indicate the existence of assets. For example, repeated travel to a particular location may indicate business interests or assets owned there. Checks payable to a utility company may relate to a piece of real estate owned. A check to an appraiser or a title company also could suggest the existence of real estate.

Look for instances in which cash seems to disappear into thin air. Cash withdrawals (including counter and ATM withdrawals), cash received back when depositing checks, and the sale of assets with no paper trail or deposit to known bank accounts are all suspicious.

Credit Reports

Credit reports provide a wealth of information about individuals and their financial histories. The credit reports include current and previous employers, addresses, and credit accounts including real estate loans, automobile loans, and credit cards. Limits and balances on those credit accounts might provide hints about credit usage, potentially signaling hidden assets purchased on credit now or in the past. Bankruptcies, tax liens, and judgments will also be found on a credit report, and an analysis of the source documents related to them may provide information on assets owned.

Database Searches

Searches of databases can reveal clues to hidden assets. While there are databases available to consumers on the Internet, these are not usually as comprehensive as the databases private investigators can access. A simple database search is not likely to uncover a well-hidden asset, but clues may exist in the search results that lead the private investigator down a path to discovery.

Detailed Accounting Records

Detailed accounting records related to personal or business financial matters can provide hints to the ownership of assets. See Chapter 12 for a discussion of the analysis of accounting records.

Miscellaneous Records

Creativity can be helpful when looking for clues to the existence of assets. Miscellaneous records that might provide useful details include:

- Telephone records
- E-mails
- Photographs
- Personal and business calendars
- Social media posts

Overlooking Assets

In a divorce action, a number of assets may not be hidden; rather, they are overlooked because of their unusual nature. Spouses simply forget these assets exist or do not appreciate the substantial value that such assets may have, individually or collectively.

- Capital loss carryover and net operating loss (NOL) carryover—Capital losses in excess of allowable amounts may be carried over from year to year on personal income tax returns. The carryover provides tax benefits in future years by reducing taxable income in those years.
- Cemetery plots—A cemetery plot or equivalent is often purchased during a marriage, so the divorce action should address this item.

- Club memberships—A membership in a country club or golf course often requires a sizable initiation fee, which should be considered in the divorce.
- Collections and memorabilia—Valuable collectibles such as coins, stamps, comic books, antiques, books, art, or sports memorabilia can have substantial value. Examples to consider include baseball cards, NASCAR merchandise, football gear, silverware, shot glasses, model airplanes, Beanie Babies, cameras, Precious Moments figurines, coins, antiques, Waterford crystal, Swarovski crystal, wall hangings, quilting, woodworking, crafting, and collector cars. It is not uncommon for a spouse to amass large quantities of these items.
- Household items—Typical household items, such as power tools or kitchen gadgets, can have value that should be evaluated by the spouses.
- Gifts between spouses—Gifts given prior to the marriage are typically separate property, whereas gifts given during the marriage are marital property. The spouses should attempt to recall the substantial gifts so they may be divided in the divorce.
- Income tax refunds—Overpayments of personal income taxes should be considered assets in the divorce.
- Intellectual property—Copyrights, patents, and trademarks can have substantial value in the future, even if they have not historically generated income or appeared to have value.
- Life insurance policies—Whole life insurance policies have cash value that should be divided in divorce.
- Loans receivable—Funds loaned to friends, family members, or business associates should be included as assets in a divorce settlement.

Retaining Professionals

Which professional provides the right services in the family law case? A variety of professionals with a wide range of expertise in financial matters is available, and it is important to choose carefully. As it relates to uncovering hidden assets, the following are the three most important professionals to consider and their areas of expertise:

- Private investigators are adept at identifying hard assets such as real estate, vehicles, aircraft, and boats. They also perform background checks on businesses and individuals, which could reveal relationships ultimately pointing to hidden assets.
- Title companies perform title searches and verify ownership of real estate.
- Forensic accountants are often best at tracing funds through known bank and brokerage accounts to look for clues to additional accounts or assets that have not been disclosed.

Chapter 11

Special Items in Lifestyle Analysis

As with most of the work done by forensic accountants, the results of the lifestyle analysis can be skewed if "special" items are not treated correctly. Various cash receipts and expenditures of money by the family can have an impact on the calculations. Statutes, their interpretations, and case law may provide little to no guidance on the special items, since it is rare that the family lawyer encounters them.

In this chapter, we address some of the special situations that can occur in a divorce and will impact the lifestyle analysis. As with all of the material in this book, your local rules must be considered and will take precedence over any guidance offered here.

Nonstandard Forms of Compensation

Executive compensation plans often compensate employees in a number of ways considered nonstandard. In other words, they are different than the typical wages, commissions, and bonuses we usually see in divorce and child support cases. These other types of compensation can be valuable, so it is important to inquire as to their existence. It is not safe to assume that just because the spouse has not mentioned another form of compensation, it does not exist.

There may be a tendency to exclude nonstandard forms of compensation from consideration in the lifestyle analysis simply because they are unusual and potentially difficult to understand. However, these items of compensation all have value, so it is imperative that they be considered in the lifestyle analysis. They must be included in support calculations and may factor into the asset division as well.

Commissions and Bonuses

Employees whose compensation is heavily weighted toward unpredictable forms, such as commissions and bonuses, create special issues in family law cases. The spouse paying support will often suggest that high earnings were unusual and will not be replicated. Thus, the spouse contends that support should be calculated based on a lower number. Earnings can be impacted by general economic conditions, changes in an industry, changes in the operations of the employer, and more.

The unpredictability should not deter the financial expert from attempting to calculate the reasonable level of earnings that should be used to calculate support. However, it is important to understand if commissions or bonuses have any seasonal or cyclical nature. The longer the history the expert examines, the better he or she can understand whether there is any pattern or predictability to the income.

Employee Stock Purchase Plans

An employee stock purchase plan (ESPP) allows an employee to purchase shares of a company's stock at a discount that could be as much as 15 percent below the market price. Payroll deductions are used to make contributions, which are accumulated until the purchase date. Some plans have tax advantages like 401(k)s, while others do not. The biggest advantage to a program like this is the profits that can be made when the stock is eventually sold. Because the stock was originally bought at a discount, there is more money to be made when the shares are sold.

Stock Options

Stock options can be one of the most confusing forms of income in a family law case. They can be very valuable, which is why it is important to understand them and their impact on the assets and income. A stock option gives the owner the right to purchase shares of stock at a fixed price (often discounted) during a fixed period of time.

Three types of stock options may be granted to employees:

- Qualified stock options allow the profits from the sale of stock acquired through the exercise of stock options to be taxed as capital gains income.
- Incentive stock options are a type of qualified stock option granted only to employees of a corporation. Incentive stock options enjoy favorable tax treatment but have several restrictions associated with them.
- Nonqualified stock options are the simplest type of stock option. They do not receive favorable tax treatment, and the gains are taxed as ordinary income when the options are exercised or have a readily ascertainable fair market value.

The following documents should be examined relative to stock options:

- Stock option plans
- Employment contracts
- Stock option grant documentation, including number of options, exercise dates, exercise prices, expiration dates, and vesting dates
- Company-provided valuation of options
- Benefits statements from the company
- Tax forms issued relative to the stock options

There is more than one method used to calculate the value of stock options, and state law may dictate which method is to be used. The intrinsic value method measures the difference between the strike price (which is the exercise price of the stock option) and the market value of the stock on the valuation date. The Black-Scholes option pricing method, used to value publicly traded stock options, is much more complicated.

How does a spouse ensure that he or she receives a fair portion of the value of the stock options at or after the divorce? It is important to engage a professional with substantial experience with valuing stock options, as well as one who fully understands the tax consequences of the various types of stock options. The spouses may also wish for the court to reserve jurisdiction so the value can be distributed fairly when the cash actually materializes. Although this would draw out the period of time that the finances of the spouses are intertwined, it may be the only way to ensure that the spouses share risk equally.

Restricted Stock Units
Restricted stock unit (RSU) plans are a way for a company to give stock to employees with no purchase price. There is typically a vesting period, and the grant is taxed as ordinary income in the year the vesting schedule is complete. The taxable income is the market value of the shares on the date they become vested. These shares are valuable because the employee receiving them has paid nothing. Therefore, no matter how far a company's stock price may fall, the stock granted to the employee is still worth something.

Performance Share Awards
Performance share awards (PSA) are similar to RSUs. An employee is given shares of stock based on performance measures, and the shares have a vesting schedule. Like RSUs, the award is taxable at the time the shares become vested. The taxable value is based on the market price of the shares of stock on the vesting date.

Deferred Compensation
Other types of deferred compensation, including employee stock ownership plans (ESOPs), profit sharing plans, or certain types of retirement plans, must be considered in the divorce. Typical retirement plans include 401(k), 403(b), Simplified Employee Pension (SEP), and Savings Incentive Match Plan for Employees (SIMPLE).

A high-level executive may also be offered a Supplemental Executive Retirement Plan (SERP) from his or her employer on top of the company-wide retirement plan in which the executive participates. Under the SERP, the company contributes money to a retirement plan, and the money will be taxable when the retired executive receives funds. This type of benefit is often used to reward and retain executives while not creating a taxable event until retirement.

The taxation of these deferred compensation plans varies, and often the amount of compensation to be received in the future is unknown. Regardless of the unknowns, these plans must be scrutinized and considered in the family law case. Again, a professional with substantial practical experience with these issues should be retained. It may be necessary to value a pension or other retirement vehicle, and someone with substantial experience doing these types of valuations should be retained to do so.

Life Insurance

Companies may award life insurance policies as an employee benefit. Term life insurance has no value other than the death benefit, but whole life insurance policies have an investment component that can make them valuable assets. The cash surrender value of a whole life insurance policy should be considered when tabulating marital assets.

The beneficiary or beneficiaries on a life insurance policy are important after a divorce. An ex-spouse may want or need to remain a beneficiary on the life insurance policy, especially if spousal support or child support will be ongoing. The life insurance policy will protect the recipient of the support payments in the event of the death of the payer.

Annuities

Annuities, investments sold by insurance companies, can provide a person with income during retirement. They often have a life insurance component to them in addition to the retirement benefit. Annuities are attractive investments because taxes are not due on the earnings of the investment until funds are withdrawn. Depending on the terms of the contract, an annuity may not be divisible in a divorce. However, it must still be valued and included in assets for the overall division.

Other Fringe Benefits

Employees often receive special perks or fringe benefits from their employers, particularly if they are top executives. The benefits could be worth tens or hundreds of thousands of dollars per year. These must be considered when dividing assets and determining support. Some of the perks commonly given to executives include:

- Club memberships
- Life insurance

- Employee discounts
- Personal use of corporate credit card
- Transportation (a company-provided vehicle, a driver, or both)
- Employer-paid parking
- Sporting event skyboxes or suites
- Personal use of company property (automobiles, telephones, computers)
- Loans (either low cost or as disguised compensation)
- Relocation expenses
- Corporate housing
- Private air travel
- Employer-paid vacations
- Travel for spouses and children
- Wealth management services
- Employer payment of employee's payroll taxes or income taxes (sometimes called "grossing up" compensation)

Nontaxable Income

Nontaxable income received by employees and investors must be considered income for the purposes of a family law case. Thus, the financial expert cannot rely only on items reported on the income tax return when making support calculations. In fact, by virtue of being nontaxable, this income may be even more valuable than other sources of income.

Business Income Issues

Certain items related to business interests owned by one or both spouses create controversy in family law cases. The net income of the business may be adjusted for purposes of calculating support and dividing assets. Exactly what those adjustments should be and how they should be done is fertile ground for dispute.

Ordinary and Necessary Business Expenses

Local rules regarding the calculation of income available for support typically allow a business owner to use funds for ordinary and necessary business expenses. Those funds are then excluded from the calculation of income available for support.

There are not standard rules for what is considered "ordinary" or "necessary," and there is a risk that the spouse who owns and operates the business will be aggressive in reducing the net profits of the business in an attempt to reduce the income available for support. The other spouse will likely claim that many of the business expenses are unnecessary or are personal in nature and are simply a ruse to reduce the amount of support paid.

The spouses may also disagree about whether it is proper to use some of the business funds to grow the business or begin new business ventures before support is calculated. Courts sometimes allow some level of reinvestment of money into a business, but a case can often be made that the investment is optional and should not be allowed to reduce the income for purposes of support calculations.

Depreciation

The courts treat depreciation of business assets, including real estate, inconsistently. Some courts allow depreciation on real estate to reduce the income available for support, whereas others disallow depreciation because it reduces the taxable income but is not an actual cash expense. Since real estate typically appreciates over the long term, some courts do not allow depreciation to reduce the income available for support, as it is not a true cost of holding the real estate.

States may also treat depreciation differently for child support versus spousal support. Depreciation may be allowed to reduce the income available for support for one but not the other.

Depreciation on furniture, fixtures, and equipment owned and used by a business will typically be allowed as a business expense that reduces income available for support. Assets such as these tend to have little value at the end of their useful lives, so they represent a true ongoing expense.

Pass-Through Entities

Entities such as partnerships, limited liability companies (LLCs), and S corporations earn income that is passed through to owners, reported to them on K-1s, and reported on their individual income tax returns. Even though an owner is entitled to a share of the entity's income, cash may not actually be distributed to the owners. Courts treat the issue of pass-through income differently.

The issue is further complicated by owners of entities who purposely do not distribute income in an attempt to influence calculations in the family law case. Not distributing cash may bolster claims that income does not exist.

It is important to ensure that distributions are treated consistently in the divorce case. The spouse should not be allowed to forgo distributions now to reduce support without including future distributions in support calculations.

Businesses with Losses

Sometimes legitimate business ventures suffer losses year after year. Other times, a spouse has a hobby that is disguised as a business in order to take tax deductions for the losses. In either case, the financial expert must determine how to treat the losses in the lifestyle analysis.

The Internal Revenue Service recognizes activities with recurring losses as activities not engaged in for profit. While tax rules do not always rule the day when it comes to support calculations, they can be instructive when determining how to treat the items in the financial analysis.

The "hobby loss" rules of the Internal Revenue Code limit the ability of taxpayers to use losses to reduce their overall taxes. To deduct expenses, the taxpayer must engage in or carry on an activity with an actual objective of turning a profit. There must be an honest belief that the business will turn a profit in the future.

The Internal Revenue Service usually assumes a profit motive if the business is profitable for at least three years of a consecutive five-year period. If there are not profits in at least three years, the taxpayer will have to prove the intent. Treasury Regulation § 1.183-2 sets forth nine factors that may be evaluated to determine if someone has an honest profit motive:

(1) The manner in which the taxpayer carries on the activity
(2) The expertise of the taxpayer or his or her advisors

(3) The time and effort expended by the taxpayer in carrying on the activity

(4) The expectation that assets used in the activity may appreciate in value

(5) The success of the taxpayer in carrying on other similar or dissimilar activities

(6) The taxpayer's history of income or losses with respect to the activity

(7) The amount of occasional profits, if any, that are earned

(8) The financial status of the taxpayer

(9) Elements of personal pleasure or recreation

The regulations explain each of these elements. It may be helpful to evaluate a business using this criterion before determining how to treat the venture in the family law case.

A case can be made that a spouse should not be able to use a hobby or a fake business to create losses and reduce income available for support. If this is what the spouse is attempting to do, the "business" venture should be excluded from income calculations. If it is not so clear cut, it may not be as easy to determine what to do with the losses. In the event that losses are excluded from income calculations, be aware that if the venture later turns a profit, that income may also be excluded from income and support calculations.

Division of Liabilities

The liabilities accumulated during a marriage must be divided in the divorce, just as the assets are divided. However, dividing liabilities can become complicated for a variety of reasons. First, it is important to ensure that all liabilities are identified. Second, it is imperative to understand that even if the spouses agree on a division of the liabilities, the creditors are not bound to accept the agreement. Typically, the taxing authorities will not accept an agreement on the division of tax liabilities and will pursue both spouses for unpaid taxes, penalties, and interest. Other creditors, such as banks and credit card companies, often will not accept a division of the liabilities either. Instead, the spouse who intends to assume the liability will usually have to refinance the debt, putting it in his or her name alone.

An unpaid joint debt is always a risk to both spouses. What if the spouse who assumes the debt does not make timely payments? This oversight could damage the other spouse's credit rating and may cause the creditor to pursue both spouses for payment of the liability.

Income Tax Issues

Contentious divorces can lead to allegations of cheating on income taxes and threats to report the spouse to the authorities. Even though the thought of an evil spouse getting skewered by the Internal Revenue Service may be tantalizing, there are often unintended consequences.

It is important to remember that unpaid taxes, interest, and penalties often come before other debts when a person is unable to pay them all. That is, the taxing authorities will rally hard to garnish and levy until the taxes are paid in full, regardless of whether support obligations exist. It is therefore often not advisable for the recipient of support payments to report the spouse to the taxing authorities. Which is more important: creating financial trouble for the spouse or receiving timely support payments?

Also, a spouse considering reporting the other spouse to the tax police should think carefully about his or her own involvement in the alleged tax fraud. Did both spouses know? Should both spouses have known? When a family lives a $300,000-per-year lifestyle but only reports $50,000 per year on their income taxes, serious questions may be raised about the knowledge and participation of the parties. Ultimately, *both* spouses could end up responsible for unpaid taxes, interest, penalties, and maybe even criminal charges.

It is possible for one spouse to report the other spouse for income tax fraud, possibly receiving immunity from prosecution or some other favorable treatment in exchange for providing information and documentation to the Internal Revenue Service. However, protection for the reporting spouse is never guaranteed, so the decision to report tax fraud to the authorities should never be taken lightly.

Even though innocent spouse relief is available for the spouse who is unaware of unreported income or improper deductions (which lead to income tax liabilities), it is not a guaranteed "out" for the spouse. Relief may be granted under three possible scenarios:

- Innocent spouse relief—A spouse can be relieved of all or part of a liability arising from an erroneous understatement of tax due to unreported income, improperly reported income, or improperly claimed deductions or credits.
- Separation of liability relief—A spouse's liability for a tax deficiency can be limited based on an allocation of items on the income tax return as if the couple had filed separate returns. This option may be available if the spouse is no longer married to the person with whom the joint return was filed or has been legally separated or living apart for at least 12 months. This option is not available if the Internal Revenue Service can prove that assets were transferred between spouses as part of a fraudulent scheme.
- Equitable relief—If funds intended for payment of tax on a joint income tax return were not paid with the return but were taken by the spouse for his or her own benefit, the other spouse may qualify for equitable relief if he or she had no knowledge the funds were being taken. The spouse must show that it would be unfair to hold him or her responsible for the underpayment.

Refuting the Lifestyle Analysis

While a financial expert may be retained to proactively complete a lifestyle analysis in a divorce case, one might also be retained to confirm or refute the analysis of an expert retained by opposing counsel. The process is no different than if the lifestyle analysis is being done proactively. Income and expenses are tabulated, categorized, and allocated using the methodology described in this book.

The analysis done by the expert refuting the original lifestyle analysis will likely need to be compared and contrasted to the original lifestyle analysis. However, this is not always possible. It is not uncommon for an opposing expert to provide a lifestyle analysis that includes little explanation. It is not uncommon for the lifestyle analysis to be done in a way that makes it impossible to deconstruct the analysis or point out errors in methodology or logic.

It is most important that a forensic accountant be able to thoroughly explain his or her analysis and the basis for the opinions. If he or she can adequately support his or her own opinions, the ability to explain the faulty analysis of the opposing expert will become much less important.

Chapter 12

Business Lifestyle Analysis

Closely held businesses present special challenges in the family law setting. Typically, only one spouse is actively involved in the business. Therefore, not only does the spouse control the family's finances, but he or she also controls all of the records of the business. When the spouse who does not work actively in the business attempts to quantify the income from the business or the value of the business, the spouse who works in the business daily can purposely (and often very effectively) obstruct efforts to get accurate and complete data.

Certain types of businesses, such as restaurants and retail stores, can be prone to manipulation because they have so many cash transactions. Construction companies, real estate ventures, and auto dealerships are notorious for "creative" bookkeeping. Professional service providers, such as doctors, dentists, and attorneys, are at risk for financial maneuvering because it is so difficult to verify the amount of professional services actually provided to patients or clients.

Any closely held business having finances that are easily manipulated by the owner is at risk. If this happens, the "out" spouse is left looking for alternatives to get to the bottom of the finances. Techniques used in the personal lifestyle analysis can also be applied to businesses to ferret out the truth about the money.

Business Types

A business entity may take one of four forms—sole proprietorship, partnership, limited liability company (LLC), or corporation.

Sole Proprietorship

The sole proprietorship is the most basic form of business, with one owner and no formal business structure. The individual could do business under a separate name, often called a fictitious name or DBA (doing business as). Some state and local governments require registration of sole proprietorships, and there may also be rules related to registering fictitious names. A sole proprietorship will file its taxes as part of an individual's income tax return, Form 1040, Schedule C (Profit or Loss from Business).

One typical problem with sole proprietorships is the tendency of the owner to commingle personal and business funds. Business accounting records may not be kept very well, making a financial analysis of the business difficult. Sole proprietorships are often run less formally than the other business types, and sometimes sole proprietorships are not really business ventures. It is important to determine the true nature of the operations.

Partnership

A partnership (sometimes referred to as a general partnership) is formed with an agreement between two or more people. Profits and losses may be split by the owners equally, in proportion to their ownership percentages, or in some other agreed-upon proportion. Like sole proprietorships, partnerships do not always have to be registered with state or local governments. Rules differ among jurisdictions. Income and expenses are reported for income tax purposes on Form 1065 (U.S. Return of Partnership Income), and each partner is issued a K-1 to document his or her share of the partnership income or loss.

When investigating a partnership, it is not enough to see only a partner's K-1. The K-1 provides only summary information. The entire income tax return is needed to understand and evaluate the line items contributing to the bottom-line profit or loss.

Limited Liability Company

A limited liability company (LLC; sometimes incorrectly referred to as a limited liability corporation) is a form of business similar to a corporation in many ways. The LLC is theoretically easier to administer than a corporation, and business owners use this form of business because it is easy to file the initial paperwork.

An LLC may be treated like a partnership for income tax purposes, filing Form 1065. Alternatively, it may elect to be treated like a corporation for income tax purposes, filing Form 1120. One person can form a single-member LLC and, in that case, would file Schedule C of Form 1040 to report business income or loss.

Corporation

A corporation registers with a state and issues stock to its shareholders. It may file Form 1120, U.S. Corporation Income Tax Return, or Form 1120S, U.S. Income Tax Return for an S Corporation. It is important to investigate whether a corporation has any subsidiaries or is part of any joint ventures, partnerships, or other corporations. Those ownerships and involvements can substantially affect the value of a corporation.

Documents to Analyze

Chapter 6 introduced us to some of the documents that can be analyzed relative to business interests, and Appendix B provides a detailed list of documents that may be requested during discovery. Note that there may be unusual situations that are not addressed by the list.

When a closely held business is being evaluated in connection with a family law case, the following business-related documents may be requested:

- Business ownership records (stock certificates, charters, operating agreements, joint venture agreements, corporate minutes, or other related documents)

- Business income tax returns (Form 1065, 1120, or 1120S) for any business in which the spouse/parent has had an ownership interest for the last five years
- Books of minutes for companies controlled directly or indirectly by the party, including articles of incorporation, amendments, bylaws, minutes, and resolutions of shareholders and directors
- Financial statements for any business entity in which there has been an interest, including professional practices, joint ventures, and co-ownerships, for the last five years
- Copies of valuations or appraisals done within the preceding five years
- Copies of budgets, forecasts, projections, or business plans prepared within the preceding five years
- List of all bank accounts in the company's name, including the bank name, bank location, account number, and type of account
- List of all bank accounts in the company's name that have been closed within the last five years, including the bank name, bank location, account number, and type of account
- Copies of all applications for credit made with banks, mortgage brokers, or any other financial institution in the preceding three years
- Copies of all bank statements, checks, deposit slips, and wire transfers for the last three years
- Copies of all credit card statements for the last three years
- Copies of all brokerage account statements for the last three years
- Access to detailed accounting records, including the general ledger, general journal, sales journal, purchases journal, cash receipts journal, cash disbursements journal, and subsidiary ledgers
- List of names, addresses, and ownership percentages of all shareholders

This list is not all-inclusive. It is the starting point and contains some of the most common documents that will be requested for a business. However, other items can be obtained depending on the issues in a particular family law case.

As always, the most reliable records are third-party documents, such as bank statements and credit card statements. These are nearly impossible to manipulate, and if obtained directly from the third party, the data is reliable. These statements will tell the truth about where the money moved to and from.

Bank statements and credit card statements might show a picture different from the one that has been reported by the spouse in financial disclosures, income tax returns, or financial statements. Bank deposits may show a higher level of revenue than the business has reported. Although people who are attempting to conceal revenue usually do not deposit all cash receipts to the bank, it is still important to analyze the deposits in the event they contain some useful information.

The attorney should call on the financial expert for assistance with the discovery process. Not only can the expert provide insight into the documents that should be requested, but he or she can also evaluate what is produced to determine if it is fully responsive to the demands that were made. For example, opposing counsel may provide only certain pages of an income tax return and refuse to provide the remaining pages. The financial expert can explain exactly what those pages are, the forms or schedules contained within them, and why the missing pages must be produced.

Accounting Records

Detailed accounting records, such as the general ledger and supporting documentation, may be necessary to determine whether:

- A spouse has used business funds to pay personal expenses
- Income and expenses of the company are legitimate or manipulated
- Key customers or vendors are engaging in legitimate transactions with the company
- Any large one-time expenses were incurred (which may need to be adjusted when analyzing the numbers in a divorce case)
- Assets or liabilities of the company were manipulated
- Write-offs or adjustments to the books are appropriate
- Future income and expenses can be estimated

Bank Statements, Brokerage Statements, and Credit Card Statements

If the authenticity of the accounting records is questioned or if source documentation is required to complete the financial investigation, bank statements, brokerage statements, and credit card statements are the primary source of evidence of the movement of funds. While these documents can be voluminous, they are desirable because they are not subject to manipulation and, therefore, deemed reliable evidence.

Contracts and Business Agreements

Evaluate contracts to determine the nature of the business relationship between the company and other parties. Are they related parties? Is there an arms-length business relationship? Are the parties engaging in legitimate, necessary business transactions, or are the transactions a sham? Could the transactions be used to manipulate the value of the company or the assets available for division?

Appointment Books

For service providers such as doctors, dentists, accountants, attorneys, cosmetologists, massage therapists, and automobile repair shops, appointment books can be valuable tools for verifying representations about revenue. Appointment books for current and past years should be compared to one another, and they should also be compared to the financial statements and income tax returns. Does the volume of appointments seem to correlate with the revenue reported? Has there been a change in reported revenue without a corresponding change in the volume of appointments? Do the appointment books tend to support or refute representations about the level of activity in the business?

Billing Records

In a service-based business, a look at billing records can point to hidden revenue. Billing records should be evaluated in much the same way as appointment books. Service providers such as doctors, dentists, lawyers, and accountants often have meticulous records of procedures, time spent, and costs related to patients and clients. It is more difficult to manipulate the detailed records than the summary financial statements, so the billing records may be a true reflection of the revenue.

Loan Documents

As with the personal lifestyle analysis, loan applications made by business entities can be invaluable sources of financial information. The business will be required to disclose income, assets, liabilities, and other financial information. The business will be used to confirm or refute representations made in the family law case about the financial condition of the business.

General Financial Analysis

Before we discuss what can be learned from specific income, expense, asset, and liability accounts, we will address general analysis that can be done on the financial statements. The analysis of financial statements is an important process in detecting manipulation of the financial statements. Account balances and relationships should be evaluated. How have account balances changed from period to period? How have the relationships between accounts changed from period to period?

Be aware that an analysis of financial statements can reveal things other than fraud. The analysis could find differences or unexpected changes that are a result of errors, fraud, or unusual or nonrecurring events. We cannot automatically assume that fraud is to blame for questionable results of the analytical review but must instead look for other evidence that could support or refute a claim of fraud.

Vertical Analysis

In vertical analysis, expenses on a company's income statement (alternatively called profit and loss statement) are expressed as a percentage of revenue. Some expenses rise and fall in close relation to revenue, whereas others move independently of revenue. The expert evaluates these percentages for multiple periods to understand changes and possibly identify irregularities.

In the example on the next page, we have calculated each line item as a percentage of sales. This makes it easier to compare companies of varying sizes, and it allows us to see how the numbers relate to sales over time.

Tax Return Summary
JLC LLC

	2018	Percent of Sales
Sales	$6,550,000	
Cost of Goods Sold	4,380,000	66.9%
Gross Profit	$2,170,000	33.1%
Salaries & Wages	$ 680,000	10.4%
Repairs & Maintenance	12,000	0.2%
Rent	48,000	0.7%
Taxes & Licenses	21,500	0.3%
Interest	63,000	1.0%
Depreciation	180,000	2.7%
Other Expenses	80,000	1.2%
Total Expenses	$1,084,500	16.6%
Net Income	$1,085,500	16.6%

Horizontal Analysis

In horizontal analysis, the expert compares financial statement data over multiple periods. Comparisons may be made between months, quarters, or years. Accounts analyzed between periods typically include the revenue accounts and the larger or more risky expense accounts.

The forensic accountant looks at the changes between periods, in terms of both dollar changes and percent changes. Irregularities identified during this analysis may guide some of the work performed in the lifestyle analysis.

In the example on the next page we have put the tax return data in columns next to one another to allow an easy comparison from year to year. In addition to looking at dollar changes over time, we examine percentage change between periods.

Tax Return Summary
JLC LLC

	2016	2017	2018
Sales	$2,470,000	$3,520,000	$6,550,000
Cost of Goods Sold	1,748,000	3,011,000	4,380,000
Gross Profit	$ 722,000	$ 509,000	$2,170,000
Salaries & Wages	$ 195,000	$ 340,000	$ 680,000
Repairs & Maintenance	20,000	2,500	12,000
Rent	36,000	36,000	48,000
Taxes & Licenses	23,000	19,000	21,500
Interest	34,000	46,000	63,000
Depreciation	121,000	70,000	180,000
Other Expenses	40,000	65,000	80,000
Total Expenses	$ 469,000	$ 578,500	$1,084,500
Net Income	$ 253,000	$ (69,500)	$1,085,500

Ratio Analysis

Forensic accountants have a number of ratios that they may calculate to further evaluate the financial statements. Numerous ratios can be calculated relative to revenue, cost of goods sold, accounts receivable, inventory, and more. These ratios help evaluate the business, compare it to other companies in the same industry, and look for irregularities in the financial statements.

Income statement ratios provide information about the profitability of a company. If a company's sales are actually increasing or decreasing, certain other accounts should be moving in a predictable manner too. When those other accounts are not changing as expected, this calls into question whether the sales figures are being reported accurately.

Balance sheet ratios can speak to the financial health of a company. When evaluating business finances in a divorce, unusual balance sheet ratios may point to fraud. Manipulation of revenue can impact the balance sheet, so strange balance sheet ratios may point to such problems.

Evaluating Income

A company's current income should be compared to historical income, and the reasons for any changes over time should be determined. Any substantial one-time sales that will not recur (or will recur only infrequently) should be considered when projecting future income.

It is not unusual for the revenue of a closely held business to drop dramatically around the time of the filing of a family law case. The spouse who is active in the business may attempt to make it appear as if the business is failing. A failing business has a lower value to be divided between the spouses, and a failing business also means there is less income from which support can be paid.

The financial expert should consider whether the income of the company has fallen because a new subsidiary or related third party has been created to receive the income. This could be an attempt to shield income from the family law case or otherwise deprive a spouse of a share of assets or income.

If income has gone down after the filing of the family law action, related expenses should be evaluated to determine if they have decreased proportionately. This is discussed in more detail in the next section of this chapter.

An analysis of revenue by customer should be completed to determine if any long-term customers have disappeared from the accounting records. It is possible that those customers are still purchasing from the company, but the revenue is not being recorded in the financial statements.

Cash businesses can be especially difficult to investigate. They include those that traditionally deal with higher volumes of cash, such as restaurants, bars, gas stations, convenience stores, fitness studios, laundromats, landscapers, salons and spas, and other retail stores. Certainly, there has been a shift to payments with credit cards and debit cards, but in some of these businesses, a substantial percentage of business is still transacted with cash.

A few of the more common techniques for verifying income in cash-intensive businesses include:

- Compare the revenue collected in cash versus credit cards. Examine both the raw dollars and the relative percentages of cash to credit cards. Unusual changes over time may indicate the failure to report cash collections.
- Research the normal mark-up or profitability of the product or service sold, and determine how the figures of the company compare. For example, if purchase records for a gas station are available, the fuel volume times the average price equals estimated gross receipts. The estimated gross receipts can be compared to reported receipts from fuel sales.
- Identify expenses that move in a predictable fashion with income, and see if any anomalies exist across years.
- Find a documented expense that could prove or disprove income. For example:
  - A laundromat reports a substantial decrease in income after the filing of divorce. Water bills show that the water usage has not decreased. This may tend to show that income is intentionally underreported.
  - Shipping records from a private company such as UPS or FedEx may show that the volume of packages shipped by a business has not decreased, even though income is allegedly down.
  - Purchases of alcohol for a restaurant or bar may show no changes in quantities, despite the business reporting substantially reduced income.
- Examine payroll records to determine if staffing has been reduced after a claimed decrease in income.
- Compare the lifestyle of the business owner to the reported income. Is the income sufficient to support the lifestyle? If not, are there other sources of funds that could be used to fund the lifestyle? If the cost of the lifestyle exceeds the reported income of the business and no other apparent source of funding exists, it is possible that revenue has been underreported.

Evaluating Expenses

There is a tendency to gloss over business expenses and assume they are legitimately incurred in the normal course of business. This is not necessarily the case, and inflated business expenses can reduce business profits. This would cause a valuation of the business to be lower than it ought to be, which could negatively affect a spouse during divorce.

It is not uncommon for a business owner to pay personal expenses with business funds, and this is discussed in greater detail later in this chapter. The forensic accountant should consider whether expenses have a true business purpose, as these personal expenses can accumulate to a material sum of money. For example, the owner of a company may have the company purchase an automobile for his use, although he has no business need for it. As another example, the owner may secretly create an entity that receives substantial payments from the original company for "consulting." This may be an attempt to reduce the profitability of the original company, which can affect business valuation and the division of assets.

The financial expert may ultimately adjust several items in the business financial statements to bring the numbers in line with those of a company with financial statements not subject to the whims of an owner. Even small adjustments to several line items could collectively alter the financial picture of the company.

Automobiles

Deductions for the business use of automobiles are often abused. Even if the letter of the law is followed, the deduction of automobile expenses can reduce the profits of a business unfairly. This misuse is especially significant if related to a luxury vehicle, with no good reason for the business to incur such an expense.

It is important to understand the tax rules for deducting automobile expenses to know what is valid. A valid deduction for a vehicle relates only to the business use of that vehicle. If a car is used for both personal and business purposes, the business should be paying for only the business portion of the expenses. Business use does not include commuting between home and the business site. Does the employee use the automobile to travel to client sites? In the case of sales or service employees, this is likely. In the case of executives, it is often questionable. Dig into whether the owner or employee is using the vehicle for bona fide business purposes or is instead causing the business to pay for a car for which there is no legitimate business need.

The financial expert should examine the number of vehicles being deducted by the business and look at the method of calculating the deduction:

- The business may purchase or lease the vehicle for the employee or owner and pay some or all of the cost.
- The employee or owner may purchase or lease his or her own vehicle, and the company may reimburse the actual cost of operating the vehicle using either a standard mileage rate or the actual expense method.
- The employee or owner may purchase or lease his or her own vehicle, and the company reimburses him or her using a standard rate per mile driven.
- The company may provide the employee or owner with a monthly automobile allowance to be used for vehicle expenses.

Any one of these four methods may result in excess reimbursement for the employee or owner, whereby he or she receives more money or a greater benefit than the actual business usage of the automobile.

It is also common for a spouse or child of an owner or executive to have use of an automobile paid for by the company. There is likely no legitimate business purpose for doing so. This issue should be evaluated, and the financial statements should be adjusted to remove nonbusiness expenses prior to using those statements for support calculations or business valuations.

The forensic accountant should look for evidence of business usage of the vehicle, especially mileage logs (which are required to be kept under Internal Revenue Service rules). Consider adjusting the company's vehicle expense to properly reflect the business use of a reasonable vehicle that is necessary to the business. Other automobile expenses may simply be perks that should be considered compensation.

Bad Debt Expense

When bad debts (accounts receivable that cannot be collected) are written off at rates higher than normal, it is cause for concern. Write-offs could be related to the state of the economy or the health of the business, but they could also be an attempt to look less profitable or devalue the company.

Bad debt expense should be examined, focusing on:

- Whether the rate of write-offs has changed
- Whether there is an increase in the amount of write-offs or the size of accounts being written off
- Whether bad debts are being written off at the same age as in the past
- The industry practice for writing off bad debts
- Whether reasonable efforts have been made to collect the debts
- Whether payment may have been made on the debts, but the cash has been diverted or concealed

If a bad debt is legitimately written off, the company will almost certainly stop doing business with the customer. If the company continues to book revenue from the customer, this suggests that the write-offs were really not bad debts.

Consultants

Consultants are routinely retained in the ordinary course of business to complete projects for companies. However, owners and management can abuse "consulting expense." This line item may be used to conceal compensation to the owner or related parties or to otherwise funnel money to the owner without users of the financial statements knowing who truly received the funds.

The details behind consulting expenses should be examined. Contracts or other documentation that outlines the scope of work, parties performing the work, and compensation for the work are valuable. If it appears that consulting work did not occur or that the payments are a form of disguised compensation or money transfers, the forensic accountant should consider an adjustment to the financial statements.

Cost of Goods Sold

Unexplained increases in the cost of goods sold may be an attempt to manipulate business financial statements. This will ultimately affect a business valuation and support calculations. The financial expert should examine the cost of goods sold in dollars as well as the cost of goods sold as a percentage of revenue. If the cost of goods sold as a percentage of revenue has changed substantially, reasons for the changes should be considered.

Increases in cost of goods sold should be evaluated skeptically. If raw materials or other supply costs have allegedly increased, this increase should be verified with source documentation. Any new suppliers should be evaluated to determine whether they are legitimate suppliers or a sham used to divert company funds.

Depreciation

Depreciation can be a complicated part of the company's financial statements. Income tax laws allow a business to deduct depreciation in an accelerated manner. This gives a larger deduction in earlier years, which may unfairly reduce the net income of the business for purposes of a business valuation or other divorce calculation.

Additionally, the book value of assets (cost less accumulated depreciation) may not reflect the true value of the assets to the business. For example, a fully depreciated asset will show a book value of $0, but the asset may still contribute substantially to the business. Therefore, the value of that asset to the company is much greater than the book value of $0.

Adjustments to depreciation are often made for business valuations and other calculations for family law cases.

Employees

Parties related to the owners or executives of a company (such as children, spouses, or significant others) may receive compensation as employees of the company. Two problems may arise with these arrangements. The employees may not be performing work on behalf of the company, and they may be compensated simply as a benefit to the owner or executive. Alternatively, the employees may actually work for the company but may be paid at a rate that is much higher than market rates.

The forensic accountant should determine the nature of the work performed by the employee and research market wages for the job. An adjustment to the financial statements should be made for compensation that does not appear to be in line with market rates for unrelated parties.

Insurance

Even though insurance is usually a legitimate business expense, it could also be a perk to owners and executives that is disguised as a business expense. The financial expert should examine insurance policies to determine what insurance policies the company is funding and whether the insurance expense is a reasonable and necessary business expense. It should also be determined whether there are assets being insured by the business that have not been disclosed in the divorce previously. It is also important to note that whole life insurance policies may have a cash value that should be considered when evaluating assets in a divorce case.

Interest Expense

Interest expense related to a business loan, line of credit, or credit card can be a legitimate business expense, but it may also be abused. The forensic accountant should investigate the identity of the creditor and examine documents evidencing the debt, such as a loan agreement. The expert should verify that the company received the funds at the inception of the loan.

Determine whether the creditor is a legitimate lender and an unrelated third party. If the creditor is a related party with a special interest in the debt, the interest expense may need to be adjusted. Consider whether the loan is really a sham transaction that was done to allow the company to make "interest payments" to a party for personal reasons. This may be an attempt to conceal the true nature of a transfer of funds to a related party. It may also unfairly reduce the net income of the company.

Miscellaneous Expenses

Catch-all categories of expenses such as "miscellaneous expenses" should be evaluated to determine whether they are used to conceal the true nature of expenses or to inflate business expenses (to lower overall profitability).

Nonrecurring Expenditures

Large expenditures, including asset purchases or expenses incurred, should be examined to determine:

- The business purpose of the expenditure
- Whether the expenditure is expected to recur
- How the expenditure was booked for income tax purposes and financial statement purposes
- The estimated useful life of the asset or the periods benefitting from the expenditure

The financial expert should determine whether an adjustment should be made to the financial statements for accelerated depreciation or other expensing of an item, which may not reflect the true use of or benefit from the expenditure. In other words, if the expenditure benefits future periods, the cost should probably be spread over those periods.

Rent

Rental payments are sometimes used to disguise payments to related parties. Rent expense may be recorded for premises that are not actually rented, or above-market rent may be paid for leased space. A business owner may pay rent to himself or herself for a portion of a residence when there is no legitimate need for office or storage space at the residence.

Examine leases to determine what space is being rented, the rental rates being paid, and the ownership of the property. Compare the rental rates to publicly available information on market rental rates for similar properties. As with other questionable business expenses, the financial expert may consider an adjustment to the financial statements if rental payments are determined to be inflated or illegitimate.

Repairs and Maintenance

It is not unusual for a closely held business to record repair and maintenance expenses unrelated to company business. Repairs, landscaping, renovations, and additions to the private residence or investment property owned by the company's owners or executives could be included in the company's financial statements.

The forensic accountant should examine these repair and maintenance expenses along with any asset additions included on the company's books to verify the nature of the expenditures and evaluate source documents such as contracts and invoices. Adjustments should be made to the financial statements for any items that are determined to be personal.

Telephone

Telephone expenses should be examined to determine whether the company is paying for personal phones belonging to owners or executives and their families. While it is quite common for companies to provide mobile phones or landlines to key personnel, this item should be evaluated to determine if the expenses recorded are necessary and reasonable.

Travel and Entertainment

An often-abused business expense relates to travel and entertainment. It is simple for an owner or executive to use a company credit card for personal meals, hotels, airfare, and entertainment. Other personal purchases could also be charged to the company credit card. It is not uncommon for the company to look the other way when such things are done, particularly if the company is closely held or the person making the charges is an owner or high-level executive.

The financial expert should conduct a thorough examination of travel and entertainment line items and adjust the financial statements if personal expenses have been included in the company's financial statements.

Wages and Salaries

The salaries and wages of owners, executives, and related parties should be examined for reasonableness. Even though wages and benefits are normal business expenses, they can be manipulated, especially in a closely held company in which the divorcing spouse is an owner or high-level executive.

The forensic accountant may have to adjust salaries to the market level that would be paid to unrelated managers or executives, sometimes referred to as a normalization adjustment. For example, an owner may fail to take a paycheck, which would inflate the bottom line profits of the business. This could affect the valuation of the business if an adjustment was not made to recognize the normal salary that would be paid for work performed by the owner.

Consider also that salaries could be abnormally high or low for a legitimate reason. For example, the owner of an S corporation may draw a lower salary, boosting the net income of the company. The owner's income includes both the salary and profits, but the salary may be paid this way as a tax-planning strategy. The accounting expert should examine wages, profits, and distributions to an owner to ensure that all avenues of income from the business are included in divorce calculations.

However, if an owner or executive reduces or eliminates his or her salary around the time of a divorce, this action could be aimed at showing that there is no income available for support. There could be an agreement or intention to withhold the paycheck now and distribute the earnings after the divorce is finalized.

The forensic accountant may also consider comparing the business owner's salary recorded on the books of the company to the deposits made to the family's personal bank accounts to determine whether the entire salary is being used for the benefit of the family. Any differences between the salary paid and the funds deposited must be reconciled.

Evaluating Assets

A company's assets are vital to its existence and could make up a substantial portion of the company's value. It is not unusual for owners or executives of closely held businesses to manipulate the assets around the time of a family law case. This manipulation may influence a business valuation, the division of property, or calculations related to support.

Accounts Receivable

An irregular decline in the accounts receivable balance of a company could be caused by writing off accounts or failing to bill customers for goods and services provided (also referred to as deferred billing). An account that has been written off actually may have been paid by the customer, with cash diverted from the company. Write-offs could also be used to make the financial condition of the company look poorer in an effort to influence a business valuation or support calculation.

Additional information on evaluating accounts receivable is contained in the Bad Debt Expense section earlier in this chapter.

Asset Additions

As mentioned previously in this chapter, it is not unusual for a closely held business to book assets that are unrelated to the company's line of business. Repairs, renovations, and additions to the private residence or other property owned by the company's owners or executives could be included in the company's financial statements.

The financial expert should examine asset additions to determine whether they are indeed assets owned and used in the ordinary course of business. The expenditures should be verified with source documents such as invoices and contracts. Adjustments should be made to the financial statements to remove any personal items.

Bank Accounts

Companies routinely utilize multiple bank accounts for a variety of different purposes. The forensic accountant should ensure that he or she has examined all bank accounts when evaluating the finances of the company. Escrow accounts and trust accounts should be examined along with the regular bank accounts used by the business.

Bank accounts may be hidden to deprive a spouse of a share of them during the division of assets in divorce. Hidden accounts may also help conceal sources of income for individuals or businesses.

If bank accounts are not disclosed (i.e., are hidden), the financial expert may uncover evidence of the accounts through an examination of transaction details. Earlier in this book, we discussed tracing funds through known bank accounts, brokerage accounts, and credit card accounts to search for evidence of undisclosed assets. Tracing funds works for the finances of individuals as well as companies.

Equipment and Furniture

As mentioned previously in the Asset Additions section, purchases of equipment or furniture for personal use could be included in a company's financial statements. The financial expert should consider evaluating fixed asset purchases to determine whether they are legitimate business expenditures.

Inventory

The forensic accountant should understand the following relative to the inventory of a company:

- The method used to value inventory
- The quantities of inventory currently on hand, and whether those quantities are in line with historical sales levels and projected sales
- Whether there have been large fluctuations in inventory, which could be related to attempts to manipulate the company's financial statements
- The level of inventory write-offs, and whether they are in line with company policy and historical write-offs

Reductions to the inventory value, including items such as spoilage, obsolete inventory, or theft, should be examined. Inventory write-offs may be manipulated to change the reported profitability or value of the business. For example, a large write-off of inventory results in higher cost of goods sold and, therefore, lower profitability. The depressed profits will cause the calculated value of the business to be lower, which will impact the division of assets.

Loans to Shareholders

Loans to shareholders may be legitimate business transactions, but they may also be used to conceal income paid to the shareholder. For example, the owner of a company may stop taking a paycheck to affect the calculation of alimony during divorce. The company may continue to pay the owner, booking the payments as "loans." Such a transaction is a sham because the owner and the company never intend for the "loan" to be repaid.

The accounting expert should evaluate the following with regard to the shareholder loans:

- The loan agreement
- The stated purpose of the loan
- The first disbursement of funds under the loan agreement
- Any subsequent disbursement of funds
- The interest rate applied to the loan
- The terms under which the loan is to be repaid
- The actual payments made by the shareholder (The lack of payments by the shareholder might suggest that the loan is not a legitimate transaction for which the company expects repayment.)

Loans made to any related third party (likely booked as "notes receivable") should be examined in the same way, as loans to other related parties may also be aimed at manipulating the value of the company.

Petty Cash

Businesses often keep small amounts of cash on hand for incidental business expenses. However, over the course of a year, the amounts that run through the petty cash account can add up. The forensic accountant should consider whether receipts have been kept for purchases allegedly paid with petty cash. It may be necessary to adjust the financial statements for items that appear to be personal rather than business-related.

Prepaid Expenses

Owners and executives of closely held companies involved in family law cases may prepay certain expenses of the business to reduce the amount of cash on the books and to manipulate the company's financial statements. The forensic accountant should look for evidence of prepayment by analyzing historical and current monthly and quarterly expenses and examining supporting documentation. If evidence of prepayment is found, the financial statements may need to be adjusted to reflect the normal pattern of incurring and paying business expenses.

Real Estate

Real estate is recorded on a company's books at cost less accumulated depreciation. Buildings will be depreciated, whereas land will not. Usually the book value of real estate does not reflect its market value. The market value will be very important when evaluating financial issues in a divorce. A real estate appraiser may be needed to properly value the real estate during divorce.

Evaluating Liabilities

The liabilities of a company are important in family law cases because they impact the value of a company and its future cash flow. Creating fictitious liabilities could reduce the value of the company, and a spouse may be deprived of his or her rightful share of the true value of the company.

Accounts Payable

Fictitious accounts payable may be created to decrease the company's profitability, inflate the company's liabilities, or both. The forensic accountant should examine accounts payable to determine:

- The identity of the creditor and whether the creditor is a related party
- Whether the creditor is a new supplier or vendor—New suppliers or vendors may be engaged in legitimate transactions with the company, or they may be sham entities used to inflate accounts payable.
- The purpose of the expenditure
- The payment terms
- Whether the products or services appear to be purchased at market rates
- Whether the debt has been satisfied but remains on the books

Notes Payable

Like loans to shareholders or notes receivable, the forensic accountant should carefully evaluate the circumstances and terms for notes payable to determine if they are legitimate business transactions or attempts to manipulate a company's financial statements.

The following items should be evaluated and verified:

- The loan agreement
- The stated purpose of the loan
- The original disbursement of funds or consideration received by the company pursuant to the loan agreement
- Subsequent receipts of funds under the loan agreement
- Terms under which the loan is to be repaid
- The interest rate on the loan
- Actual payments made on the loan—Absence of payments may indicate that the loan is not a legitimate transaction.

Evaluating Capital Accounts

Capital accounts include the investments made by owners and shareholders as well as the undistributed accumulated net income (also called retained earnings) of the business. A company's assets less its liabilities equals equity (which includes capital accounts).

Capital Investments

Owners of a company invest cash or other assets when the company is started and potentially at various times throughout the company's existence. Increases in capital accounts generally signal additional contributions of cash or other assets by the owners. The forensic accountant should evaluate the source of the funds to determine whether there are hidden assets that might impact the financial aspects of a divorce.

Withdrawals or distributions from capital accounts should also be examined, as they could be used to disguise income or divert assets. Even withdrawals believed to be legitimate should be analyzed because they may provide valuable insights. The withdrawals can point to other business interests that an owner may be a party to.

Undistributed Profits

Sometimes business owners elect to not distribute profits to themselves, and the question becomes whether those profits should still be included as income in support calculations. It is important to understand the history of distribution of profits, which might be called dividends, owner's draw, or distributions. Was there a typical amount or percentage that was distributed previously? What was the timing of the distributions before versus after the filing of divorce? Did distributions stop after the divorce filing?

Even if there does not appear to be any nefarious intent in stopping distributions, it is still important to understand why. Sometimes a case is made that the funds are needed for "reinvestment" in the business. While the reinvestment may be legitimate, the profits may still need to be considered in current income calculations.

Transfer of Ownership or Control

Business owners may attempt to transfer or sell ownership or control of a business to deprive a spouse of a portion of the assets or a portion of the income of the business. Transfers to related parties, close friends, or close business associates may suggest that the transaction is a sham. Transfers at prices well above or below market value may also indicate a sham transaction.

Looking for Red Flags

One of the most basic indicators that the numbers of a business have been manipulated is an inconsistency between documents. It is important for the forensic accountant to apply professional skepticism to documents received, constantly questioning whether the documents and numbers are authentic or manipulated.

The financial records should be evaluated not just in terms of the numbers themselves but also relative to the quality. Has the quality and completeness of financial information changed over time? Is there any explanation for the change in the quality of financial information? Could a change in the quality of information be related to a manipulation of the financial condition of the company?

In addition to all the items discussed previously in this chapter, some of the most common analyses that can uncover financial irregularities in businesses are considered next.

Costs Fluctuate with Revenue

When businesses underreport revenue, they typically make mistakes related to reporting expenses. Business owners are often eager to report all expenses, either to reduce taxable income or to manipulate income for the family law case. An analysis of expenses that normally fluctuate with revenue may uncover red flags.

In most businesses, some expenses tend to fluctuate with revenue. For example, a manufacturer of products often sees cost of goods sold correlating closely with sales. As the company sells more, it must incur more expenses in sourcing raw materials and manufacturing the product. When less is sold, the cost of goods sold tends to decrease accordingly.

The same holds true for all types of businesses. In restaurants, food costs are generally correlated to revenue. In companies providing personal services, wages and salaries for employees will often move in step with revenue. A dental practice will see materials and laboratory costs that track with revenue.

To find hidden or underreported revenue in a business, expenses that correlate with income should be isolated. Historical financial statements and income tax returns should be analyzed to determine the relationship between the revenue and expenses. For example, a particular expense may be 8 percent to 10 percent of revenue historically. That percentage can be used to predict what the current expense should be, and any significant variance should be investigated.

Current figures should be analyzed to determine the relationship between the income and expense. If there is substantial fluctuation in a period, it must be investigated further. For example, if the expense mentioned earlier is

17 percent of revenue in the current period, the reason for the increase must be evaluated. Could it be that revenue has been intentionally underreported, which has caused the expense item to be a larger percentage of revenue?

In general, a sudden increase in variable expenses that typically track with income is considered a red flag. Additional measures should be taken to investigate the revenue reported by the business.

Cash Versus Credit Sales

An analysis of cash sales versus credit sales can be useful to determine whether there may be unreported revenue. Retail stores, restaurants, and bars accept both cash and credit cards from customers and are the primary types of businesses at risk of concealing cash sales. There is often a predictable ratio of cash sales versus credit card sales, and this fact can be helpful when looking for unreported revenue.

Credit card sales are difficult to conceal, so business owners will typically report those in full while skimming cash from the business and underreporting cash sales. Since cash sales leave virtually no paper trail, they are at high risk of manipulation.

A sudden change in the ratio of cash versus credit card sales is cause for concern. If the percentage of sales via credit cards is suddenly much higher, it is possible that cash sales are being concealed.

Capital Improvements

As discussed previously in this book, it is not unusual for a spouse who runs a closely held business to claim its financial condition has declined around the time of separation or divorce. An analysis of capital improvements undertaken by the business may help evaluate this issue.

A business that is losing customers or sales volume probably does not need new capital assets. In contrast, a business that is doing well and maybe even expanding would have a good reason to add or improve buildings and equipment.

Income tax records should be evaluated to determine if new buildings, machinery, and equipment have been purchased recently. If so, the reasons behind the purchases must be investigated. Such purchases are normally a sign of a flourishing and expanding business. It may be that the old equipment needed to be replaced, but such a claim should be viewed skeptically if the owner has alleged that business is down substantially.

Capital improvements that appear to be for the purpose of expanding a business can point to hidden income. Such an item alone will not prove that there is concealed revenue, but it may be one more item in support of that theory.

Personal Expenses Paid with Company Funds

It is not unusual for the owner of a closely held business to use company funds to pay personal expenses. Some of the more common personal expenses paid by companies include health club memberships, country club memberships, personal automobiles, purchases for home offices, personal meals, and various cash items.

Depending on how the personal expenses are recorded, the net income of the company may be artificially depressed. If the payments are not reported as income to the recipient, his or her personal income will also be understated. Both the artificially depressed net income of the company and the understated personal income can have a negative impact on the spouse's finances.

Business Valuations

Business valuations are generally separate from the lifestyle analysis in divorce. However, there is occasional overlap between the two because they both require so much financial analysis. The financial statements and the income tax returns are the core pieces of financial data for the business valuation.

A thorough analysis of the underlying documents may uncover issues that would have a significant impact on the business valuation, such as:

- Unreported cash sales
- Hidden compensation to the owner (e.g., personal expenses being paid with company funds)
- Excessive perks for owners or executives
- Concealed assets or liabilities

In general, any intentional manipulation of the company's numbers to influence the value of the company may be discovered during the business lifestyle analysis. Also, do not disregard the possibility that the owner of a business may intentionally provide false information to the business valuator to decrease the stated value of the business.

An owner of a business may also persuade the spouse to abandon the idea of having the business valued by a qualified appraiser. If the owner's estimate of value is used instead, the impact on the division of assets can be dramatic.

In this sample scenario, the owner of six business entities persuaded his wife to abandon the business valuations due to the time and cost involved. His stated value of the businesses for purposes of the divorce differed dramatically from the values he reported to a bank when seeking financing.

The husband reported that the business entities were worth negative $8 million, as they owed more to banks than the entities were worth. When applying for financing, the husband reported a value of more than $22 million, a difference of more than $30 million. This emphasizes the importance of having an independent appraisal of the value of the business entities.

Double Dipping

The financial expert must be careful not to double count any earnings calculated or estimated when using the figures for the division of property and the calculation of support. The compensation of a business owner (including both wages and net income of the business) will be factored into a business valuation, and that valuation will presumably be used to divide the value of the business between the spouses.

When support calculations are being made, it is important to adjust the owner's compensation downward for any value awarded to the spouse during the property division so as not to double dip. For example, if one spouse is awarded 50 percent of the value of the business at the time of the divorce, the spouse who continues to work in the business likely cannot earn the same salary he or she earned before the division. Thus his or her expected compensation from the half of the business retained must be adjusted downward accordingly. If an adjustment is not made, the spouse retaining the business might end up paying support based on earnings that do not really exist due to the property division.

Double dipping is a common error in divorce calculations. An income-producing asset is divided between the spouses, but the full value of the asset is used in the calculations related to child support and spousal support. State law varies regarding the recognition of double dipping, and how the double dipping is treated may depend on the type of asset that is being divided.

Commingled Business and Personal Records

Sometimes business owners are not diligent in maintaining completely separate business and personal financial records. This is more commonly a problem with small, closely held businesses. In the owners' minds, they sometimes do not distinguish between personal and business funds. They may use business funds to pay personal expenses, as discussed in Chapter 9. They may also use personal funds to pay business expenses.

In family law cases, it may be difficult to separate the business and personal transactions from each other. The party involved in the business may object to a detailed analysis of business records, but to the extent that there has been commingling of funds and sloppy record keeping, the spouse should not be prohibited from examining the details behind the transactions.

It is not the spouse's fault that the party involved in the business failed to segregate funds and records. Thus, the spouse should not be penalized for the other party's commingling.

Verifying Data

Much of the work in critically analyzing a business's finances will revolve around verifying data. This includes tracing numbers to source documents, comparing and contrasting source documents, and reconciling differences.

In all of this work, there is one key to remember. As a general rule, all business transactions are recorded somewhere at least twice. This is not referring to the literal or figurative "second set of books" we hear about. Instead, it refers to the fact that almost all transactions are recorded more than once as a routine matter.

For example:

- A check is written to a vendor and recorded in the accounting software. At least three records documenting this transaction exist: the check itself, the entry in the accounting system, and the entry in the bank's records (evidenced by the bank statement).
- A customer purchases goods that are shipped. At least two records related to this transaction exist: an invoice to the customer and shipping and receiving documents.
- A doctor sees a patient and provides services. At least four records related to this office visit exist: an appointment book entry, a medical chart entry, a bill to the insurance company or patient for the services, and an entry into the accounting records for the amount billed.

When a company's books and records are suspected of being inaccurate or manipulated, the financial investigator can still find the truth because transactions have two or more ways in which they are documented. All it will take is a little creativity in determining the varying sources of records and assessing which ones are the most reliable.

Chapter 13

Reporting Findings and Testifying

After the number crunching is complete, the results are assembled into a report the attorneys and the court can understand. The expert must assume that the readers of the report have no accounting or financial background. The report must be easy to understand, with exhibits and attachments supporting the opinions set forth in the report.

The Expert's Report

In most cases, the work of the financial expert will be summarized in a written report, with selected supporting documentation attached. Occasionally a written report will not be produced, but this is not recommended. The financial issues can be complicated, and it is almost always beneficial to have the facts laid out on paper so the attorney and the judge have a roadmap of the issues.

There is no standard format for a report on a lifestyle analysis. However, it is common for experts to produce large spreadsheets detailing transactions, along with a letter report that simply states certain totals for expenditures or budgets. This is not the best way to report on the findings of a lifestyle analysis because it is difficult for the attorneys and the judge to use. It is nearly impossible for them to consider the impact of eliminating or reducing certain categories of expenditures because the gigantic spreadsheet is unwieldy. A better written report presents summaries of various categories, with appropriate detail attached in the event that a user of the report needs to examine detail and figure certain adjustments.

Report Format

The key concern in writing a report in a family law case is that it is well organized and understandable by people who have no accounting or financial background. In states that adhere to the Federal Rules of Civil Procedure, experts should refer to Rule 26(a)(2), which sets out the requirements for disclosure of expert testimony. This rule says that an expert witness must provide a signed, written report that includes:

- A complete statement of all opinions the witness will express and the basis and reasons for them
- The facts or data considered by the witness in forming them
- Any exhibits that will be used to summarize or support them
- The witness's qualifications, including a list of all publications authored in the previous ten years
- A list of all other cases in which, during the previous four years, the witness testified as an expert at trial or by deposition
- A statement of the compensation to be paid for the study and testimony in the case

Even though the expert's report should be written based on the work, observations, and opinions of the expert, it is important to determine what the attorney hopes will be in the report. Presumably, the attorney and client retain an expert for a specific purpose, which is to provide opinions on certain issues. The expert should know at the outset of the engagement the topics on which the attorney and client would like opinions rendered.

Although there is no standard format for the report of a financial expert, the following format has been used successfully in many different types of lawsuits:

- Background—This section provides a short summary of the parties to the case, the financial issues, and the engagement agreed to by the expert. It also defines the issues on which the expert was retained to opine and sets the stage for explaining the analysis the expert completed. Important dates should be noted here, along with pertinent facts that will impact the work and opinions of the expert.

- Documentation—The financial expert lists the documents and other information made available to him or her for analysis. This could be a detailed listing, or it could be more of a summary. The level of detail here may be dictated by the preferences of the attorney. It is important for the expert to appreciate the difference between documents reviewed and documents relied upon in forming expert opinions.

- Analysis—In this section, the forensic accountant will explain the information analyzed and the procedures used to evaluate the numbers. If estimates were used during the financial analysis, they should be explained here, including the reasons why estimates were made and the methodology used to create the estimates. This section could be very lengthy and detailed, especially if there is substantial analysis to be explained. It will most likely include an explanation of the methodology used and the calculations made. Accounting terminology may be used in this section if it is necessary to the opinions, but it should be clearly defined and explained so that non-accountants can understand it. Some expert witnesses intentionally provide little explanation of the opinions or calculations so the opposing expert cannot replicate their numbers. However, it is recommended that thorough explanations be provided so that the users of the report can better understand the numbers. This is especially important because the judge in a family law case may not have an accounting background. More thorough explanations can lend credibility to the expert's work and opinions.

- Opinions—The opinion section of the report is the most important, as it has the opinions of the financial expert and the reasons for those opinions. This section may also include discussions of the methodology used. Some experts use this section merely to summarize the overall opinions that have already been discussed in detail in prior sections of

the report. Again, the report format discussed here is simply a sugges-
tion, and the forensic accountant should put explanations in the sections
in which they make the most sense for the case at hand.

- Qualifications—In the qualifications section of the report, the financial
  expert outlines his or her qualifications and expertise as it relates to the
  engagement. Many times, the expert may simply state that a current
  curriculum vitae is attached to the report.
- Fees—Under the Federal Rules of Civil Procedure, an expert witness
  must disclose the fees that were paid during the course of the engagement. Some states do not require such a disclosure; however, experts
  may still include this information in the report. Some experts disclose
  only their hourly rate, whereas others disclose additional information,
  such as the fees incurred to date, the fees paid to date, and any fees
  billed but unpaid.
- Attachments—If the forensic accountant has referred to exhibits or
  attachments in the body of the report, they should be included at
  the back of the report. Often the attachments will include only the
  most important pieces of evidence or spreadsheets with detailed calculations. However, the attachments may be more voluminous if the
  financial expert believes it is important to provide substantial supporting documentation.
- Other sections—There are other possible sections of a report that will
  be based on the expert's preference. A table of contents may be included
  if the report is lengthy, as this will make it easier to locate information
  quickly. Some experts like to put an executive summary or a summary
  of opinions at either the beginning or ending of the report. This can be
  an effective way of highlighting the ultimate conclusions of the expert.

Think of each section of the report as a buildup to the opinions. One
section of the report builds on the previous section. The task is outlined,
the procedures performed are summarized, the results of the procedures
are presented, and the overall opinions are presented. This is a logical progression to the expert opinions. The more logical the progression can be,
the easier the report will be to understand.

Substance should be valued over form with reports of expert witnesses, but the format of the report is still important. A visually pleasing report with conclusions that are easy to locate and attachments supporting the opinions can be invaluable to the family law case. A report using shorter paragraphs and bullet points or lists is easier to read than the report that is primarily comprised of lengthy paragraphs. It is easier for the reader to follow information when it is broken into smaller pieces and when lists or key pieces of information are presented in bullet points.

Presenting the Numbers

What is the best way to present the lifestyle analysis numbers and details? Some financial experts write a report that provides a few numbers (such as the pre-separation monthly standard of living) with little explanation. Often a large, detailed spreadsheet is attached to the report, but it is of little use to the attorney or the court.

A better approach to the report on a lifestyle analysis includes:

- Certain relevant totals
- An explanation of how the detailed data was parsed to arrive at the totals
- Related calculations or summaries helping the user of the report understand the information or consider alternatives
- Detailed transaction listings for the most important categories of expenses
- A detailed transaction listing for the universe of transactions if requested by the user of the report

Often the detailed listing of all transactions is not useful for the reader of the report. Highlighting certain key issues can be more helpful. For example, if the spouses are disputing the amounts spent on clothing during the marriage, it may be helpful to provide a detailed listing of all of the clothing expenditures during the period under review. It may be even more helpful to provide one detailed listing for the husband and one for the wife, so the two lists can be compared and contrasted. Isolating an item of contention and providing the details for that item is much more useful than providing a gigantic spreadsheet including all transactions.

Summary tables that provide insight into certain periods of time or certain categories of spending are usually more helpful than pages of detailed transactions. If the forensic accountant uses the right software, it is easy to create reports that isolate certain time periods or situations. Each summary should not be created manually, since manual calculations leave too much room for error. Instead, the expert should have the ability to generate reports automatically, selecting the inputs (such as time period, family member who benefitted from the expenditures, or categories of spending).

By maintaining a flexible database, it is possible to provide summaries of the numbers "on the fly." There is nothing that demonstrates the expert's value to the family law attorney more than sitting in a meeting and immediately providing numbers under multiple different scenarios for the attorney. As questions are raised, the forensic accountant can provide immediate answers if he or she is using the right financial analysis software.

Reasonable Certainty

Financial expert witnesses may often say something like this in their reports: "I provide these opinions to a reasonable degree of accounting certainty." This catchphrase is intended to make it clear that the calculations and opinions are not speculative, and they are based on sound methodology. A report that does not include this type of language is not suspect, but inclusion of it adds clarity.

On the issue of reasonable certainty, Memphis divorce attorney Miles Mason says:

> In direct examination, expert witnesses have a unique status that allows them to rely upon hearsay and express opinions based on that hearsay. After laying an evidentiary foundation for financial expert

witness testimony, many lawyers may ask, "To a reasonable degree of accounting certainty, have you formed an opinion?"

Why ask the question that way? In general, most states' rules of evidence and rules of civil procedure do not require the addition of the phrase "to a reasonable degree of accounting certainty."

In medical malpractice actions, judges are used to hearing medical expert witness testimony questions posed with the inclusion of these magic words: "To a reasonable degree of medical certainty, have you formed an opinion?" Because judges are comfortable hearing these magic words as a required predicate for expert medical testimony, this phrase can serve as a highlighter for the family law judge. "Hey judge, please pay attention to this answer because this is the important stuff!"

So, what does "to a reasonable degree of accounting certainty" actually mean? It is very unlikely that any particular state court has officially defined this phrase. The definition may not really be any different than the phrase as similarly used in medical malpractice actions.

One way to define the phrase could be something like: "To a reasonable degree of accounting certainty means I am comfortable and confident in my opinion. My opinion was formed based on professional judgment and review of the information and documents I was provided. In exercise of that professional judgment, I employed a forensic accounting methodology. I performed a critical analysis of the information and documentation provided to me, and I utilized the education, training, and experience gained over my career. The result is my opinion to a reasonable degree of accounting certainty."

Most times it is impossible to have 100 percent certainty about financial issues requiring forensic accounting assistance. Historical numbers can be added and subtracted correctly and there can be certainty about them. However, other types of calculations, such as those related to future needs or estimates of the total cost of a person's lifestyle, will involve some sort of judgment. One expert may see something a different way or use a different estimate, so it is not possible to have complete certainty about such figures.

There is no hard and fast rule regarding reasonable certainty. The trier of fact will determine whether the expert's calculations are fair and supportable under the circumstances. But this can make it difficult for the expert. How certain do you have to be?

One way that an expert can support his or her calculations is by using the best available evidence. Another way to support the calculations may be through the use of multiple sources of data and multiple calculation methods.

In one case, the husband was accused of not fully disclosing his income. He had three business entities and regularly shuffled money between the entities and himself. There were questions about the tax losses generated by two of the entities and whether they were bona fide losses. A detailed analysis of his spending showed approximately $40,000 per month of personal expenditures, totaling $480,000 per year. To support this analysis, the expert looked for other ways to validate the figure.

One of the entities was generating about $500,000 per year of cash flow, and the wife knew this was the entity that funded the family's lifestyle. This seemed to support the numbers from the lifestyle analysis. Financial statements the husband sent to the bank to obtain financing for his companies also supported the calculations. Those statements, which the wife was not supposed to see, showed personal income of $600,000 per year. The estimated income of the husband was now calculated three different ways (the spending analysis, the net income of one entity, and the financial statements sent to the bank), so the $480,000 derived from the lifestyle analysis could be well supported in court.

Presenting Negative Issues

What happens when the forensic accountant has done all the calculations and has testimony that is needed, but there are problems with the case, the data, or the opinions? In some cases, if the results of the lifestyle analysis are not helpful (or even detrimental) to the case, the attorney may decide to not disclose the expert witness.

A preliminary analysis prior to the disclosure of an expert witness can be helpful in this regard. It gives counsel a chance to preview the issues before the other side finds out that an expert has been involved.

If the forensic accountant has already been disclosed as an expert, it is not quite as easy to exit the case. It is possible to withdraw the expert before he or she issues a report or provides testimony. The downside to this, however, is the other side may suspect that there were problems with your case.

It may be possible to limit the opinions the expert expresses. However, this can be tricky. What if opposing counsel delves into some of these unfavorable issues in a deposition? The expert may have to testify about those findings. Counsel could deliberately limit the scope of work to be completed by the expert witness based on the findings of the consultant, potentially shielding some of the unfavorable facts from being discovered in court.

If counsel thinks there may be issues in the numbers that will be damaging to the case, it may be preferable to retain a litigation consultant, rather than an expert witness, to delve into those issues. The consultant could later be named as a testifying expert, or a separate testifying expert could be named.

A very fine line must be walked in this situation. The expert witness should never be put in a position where he or she is being untruthful, manipulating the opinions, or deliberately ignoring or hiding unfavorable information.

Below are some of the more common negative issues that may arise in the course of working with a financial expert in a family law case, along with tips on how to best handle them.

- Missing data—Sometimes opinions must be provided even when all financial data has not been produced. Maybe there are gaps in the data because of missing statements, or maybe the other side simply refuses to turn over certain data. It is important to state clearly that any numbers calculated at this point are incomplete. The expert should do his or her best to make reasonable estimates related to the missing data. If the gaps in the data are too large, it may be best to decline to render opinions because they will be unsupportable.

- Unfavorable issues—When the case has problems, it is best to confront them directly. Sometimes the numbers do not turn out the way the attorney expected them to, or the client has done something improper with the finances. If your expert found these problems, you should assume that the other side's expert will find them as well. There is no sense in ignoring the issues or trying to hide them. The forensic accountant should present the data as best as possible, being sure to be accurate and reasonable.

- Significant estimates—The work of the financial expert often involves estimates—in some cases, a lot of estimates. This may be because there is missing documentation or unknown information about a person or an entity. Sometimes in order to move forward with the analysis, the expert needs to make estimates. The estimates should be reasonable and have a sound basis so they can be defended in court.

- Client credibility problems—What happens when an expert must rely on information from the client, but the client has not been credible in the eyes of the court? Whenever possible, the financial expert should verify information provided by the client. At the very least, the expert should determine whether the information provided by the client makes sense in light of other known facts.

- Errors in the report—Even the most careful experts will occasionally make errors in their calculations. These may include clerical errors or an incorrectly applied methodology. No matter the type of the error, the financial expert should evaluate it and make necessary corrections to the numbers.

- Inconsistent testimony—It is very important that the expert's opinions be consistent between the written report, the deposition, and the trial. Telling a different story in any one of these three immediately opens the door to credibility issues. Hopefully, conflicting testimony will be a result of new information revealed since the time the expert last testified. The financial expert must be able to explain the conflicting testimony and demonstrate why different answers were given and why that is reasonable under the circumstances.

Draft Reports

It is common for attorneys to request copies of draft reports generated by expert witnesses. They are looking for differences between the drafts and the final report. They want to know why things changed. Was new evidence produced? Did the expert make a mistake at some point? Did the expert change his or her methodology or assumptions?

This is often a contentious area. Attorneys do not want the other side to see what the preliminary numbers and opinions look like. After all, until the numbers are finalized, any early numbers probably do not matter. Yet they might matter if there is evidence that someone twisted the expert's arm to change things.

Experienced divorce attorney Miles Mason weighs in with the following advice about experts and draft reports:

> Drafts of reports can be toxic. Check your state's rules of civil procedure regarding mandatory inclusion or exclusion of draft reports in expert witness disclosure requirements. The Federal Rules of Civil Procedure have been amended so that experts are not required to produce draft reports (Rule 26(b)(4)(B)). Assuming drafts are discoverable in your state courts, what can be done?
>
> Option 1. Don't create draft reports in the first place. The client and client's attorney may legitimately need to review factual narrative summaries, data input, and key assumptions. In fact, in many circumstances, the client's attorney may legitimately suggest that the forensic accountant make certain reasonable assumptions. (If a requested assumption is unreasonable, the forensic accountant should refuse to include the assumption in any financial analysis.) It is an appropriate part of the process for the forensic accountant to ask the client and attorney to fact-check the input. Many forensic accountants may seek that initial feedback before performing the analysis.
>
> Option 2. If a draft report is created, forensic accountants should consider not sharing the analysis or spreadsheet with the client and

client's attorney unless the draft is conservative. "Conservative" means the resulting opinion (and associated number crunching) is based on judgment calls, which are easy to defend if there are any questionable areas. The best strategy to defend any financial analysis is to stay away from aggressive estimates. The CPA should be able to explain to the judge why and how every analysis can be deemed conservative by making key assumptions in the favor of the opposing party and not the client.

Option 3. If the changes between the draft report and final report have an equal number of changes increasing and decreasing the net resulting opinion, sharing the draft report may not matter. Go ahead and provide all draft reports.

What can get the financial expert in trouble, on most occasions, is appearing sketchy by failure to provide any draft reports and refusing to declare whether any ever existed. For example, "Mr. Expert, can you explain your document retention policy?" "Yes, I keep everything I need to testify." "Is your document retention policy written?" "No." "Does your unwritten document retention policy require you to maintain all of your draft reports whether or not a draft report is shown to your client and your client's lawyer?" "No." "Did you disclose any draft reports in your documents produced pursuant to the subpoena of all draft reports?" "I disclosed all of the draft reports I maintained." "I didn't ask you that. Were any draft reports sanitized from your file?" "I don't remember. I don't sanitize my files." "Did you document all of the electronic files you deleted prior to your document production in response to the subpoena?" "No." "So, under oath and subject to the criminal penalty of perjury, can you affirmatively state you have produced to me absolutely all draft reports that ever existed?" "No."

"Is it possible that after showing your client and your client's lawyer a draft report, data was changed that made your resulting opinion more favorable to your client's opinion?" "I don't remember." "You have no written document retention policy. You failed to record files you deleted. And now we can't review draft reports shown to your client and your client's attorney prior to issuing your final report in order to assess your independence and due professional care." "That is correct." "Your honor, I move to exclude this witness on the basis that the witness has violated the AICPA's Code of Professional Conduct for failure to maintain independence and exercise due professional care."

Whether or not exclusion is granted, the trial judge may see this forensic accountant as biased. Be careful with draft reports. They matter.

Using the Lifestyle Analysis

As discussed previously, the lifestyle analysis can be used to:

- Determine the standard of living (Chapter 2)
- Calculate the need of one spouse and the ability of the other spouse to pay support (Chapter 1)
- Analyze historical spending and create budgets (Chapter 8)
- Search for hidden income (Chapter 9)
- Search for hidden assets (Chapter 10)
- Evaluate closely held businesses (Chapter 12)

In addition, the lifestyle analysis may be utilized to aid in the division of property. Obviously, only assets that have been identified can be divided. Once the assets are identified, they must be valued. The relative values of assets must be compared, particularly as they relate to how liquid the assets are. Often, cash is the most valuable asset owned by the parties because all other assets carry some sort of risk in terms of the ability to turn them into cash, the amount of money it may cost to maintain them while they are owned, and the amount of cash that they will actually generate once sold.

For example, $10,000 cash may be more valuable to a spouse than a piece of artwork that is appraised at $10,000. An appraisal is no guarantee that the item can be sold for that amount, so it is important to carefully consider the relative values of assets and their liquidity. The art may also cost money to own, as it may be insured and kept in a paid storage space.

Consider $600,000 cash versus a home appraised at $600,000. The house is really only worth $600,000 if a buyer willing to pay that amount is found. In addition to a potential disparity in real values, it is important to acknowledge that a home worth $600,000 may actually be a financial drain on a spouse. Expenses such as real estate taxes, maintenance, landscaping, and insurance must be factored into any settlement scenario, as those could ultimately deplete the spouse's money. In addition, the sale of the $600,000 residence at a later date could trigger income taxes that make the asset worth "less" at the time of divorce.

These issues can and should be evaluated when potential property division scenarios are being considered. The property division should also factor into the calculations related to support. If a spouse receives assets that generate income and cash flow, there will be less of a need for the spouse to receive support. If the expert calculates support without adjusting for the income produced by the assets received, the spouse will be double dipping.

The lifestyle analysis and the expert report can also be used in practical ways in the family law case. The lifestyle analysis could be presented to an opposing expert during testimony, hopefully leading to the opposing expert making certain admissions under oath. The spouse on the other side of the case may also be presented with the expert's report and figures and may be asked to explain or refute (if he or she can) some of the expert's findings.

It may also be helpful to meet with the client and your side's financial expert at the same time. Information can be shared between the expert and client, and this may be valuable in preparing both of them to give testimony. Such a meeting may also lead to differences being worked out on some of the items. The experts can understand why their numbers differ and may end up coming to consensus on some things that were previously in dispute.

Proving Intent

In family law cases with allegations of hidden income and assets, one of the universal problems is proving intent. One of the most common defenses is that the unreported items were simply errors. It is sometimes difficult to prove that the spouse intended to underreport income and hide assets.

The forensic accountant therefore must look for characteristics of the case, the data, and the actions of the spouse that might lead a reasonable person to believe there was an intent to deceive. These might be referred to as badges of fraud and could include things such as:

- Keeping more than one set of books
- Making false accounting entries into the books and records
- Destroying documentation or other evidence
- Deleting transactions from the books and records
- Failing to disclose material financial information that would be important to the potential recipients of the information
- Making multiple misstatements and concealments, especially if there is a pattern to them
- Conducting financial business in a way so as to avoid creating a paper trail (for example, purposely using cash so there is no record of spending)
- Doing transactions in a manner that is out of the ordinary (i.e., varies from how all known financial business is done)
- Taking actions that are obvious attempts to conceal information
- Attempting to mislead users of financial data
- Denying the spouse access to documents or information necessary for the family law proceedings

The totality of the circumstances will often point toward intent. When a spouse has exhibited multiple badges of fraud that "conveniently" lead to substantial assets and sources of income being concealed in the family law case, one can reasonably infer that the spouse did not make an error but intended to conceal.

Subpoenaing the Expert's File

Following the disclosure of a financial expert, it is advisable to subpoena the expert's file. While some attorneys ask that the file be produced at the expert's deposition, it is advantageous to have the file prior to the deposition so the attorney can prepare questions about the materials in it. It is often difficult to prepare questions on the spot when receiving a file, and this is especially true if the expert brings the file in digital format and a computer is not available to view the documents.

The items to consider subpoenaing from the expert witness may include:

- A complete statement of all opinions that the expert is going to express and the basis for those opinions. If the expert has written a report, that report will likely contain those opinions. However, if no written report has been produced, it will be very important to ask for this.
- The expert's current curriculum vitae, including his or her qualifications, a list of publications authored in the last ten years, and a list of all cases in which the witness provided expert testimony in the last four years
- Reports and all drafts of reports
- All calculations and draft calculations supporting the analysis and/or serving as the basis for any of the expert's opinions
- The expert's entire file, including all materials received and/or reviewed by the expert during the course of the engagement and all work papers (both paper and digital)
- All correspondence, written or electronic, with the client, the client's attorney (and attorney's staff), the client's accountant, the client's employees, etc.
- All contracts or engagement letters evidencing the terms of the engagement
- Time and billing records for the engagement reflecting dates of service, time spent on service, and description of services performed
- A statement of compensation paid to the expert including fees billed, fees incurred but not yet billed, payments received, and billing rates for services still to be rendered (such as deposition or trial testimony)
- Any writings, reference material, articles, treatises, or books that may have served as the basis for any of the expert's opinions

There are frequently disputes over the format in which the financial expert must produce his or her work papers. The forensic accountant frequently has spreadsheets or databases that were prepared during the course of the engagement, and often the expert may want to provide only a printout of them. It is important to request that spreadsheets and databases be produced in their native format, such as the actual Microsoft Excel or QuickBooks file. The native format will make it much easier to evaluate the expert's work.

Counsel might also request information regarding prior testimony. Some attorneys simply ask for lists of depositions and trial testimony for a certain period of time. Other attorneys ask for transcripts of testimony, but the expert may not have received or retained such transcripts. The same thing may occur relative to articles or publications authored by the expert and speaking engagements done by the expert. Attorneys may ask for lists of these or for the actual articles or presentation handouts. It is common for experts to maintain lists of articles written, but they may not keep copies of the articles themselves. It is not as common for experts to keep lists of presentations made or the presentation slides or handouts.

Testifying at Deposition and Trial

Most family law cases are settled without trials. However, the attorneys must always consider the possibility of a trial and prepare the case accordingly. If the case goes far enough, the expert witness will be expected to provide testimony at deposition and trial. The expert witness has the opportunity to make or break the case for the family law attorney. The court is relying on the expert to explain the financial facts, and if the expert cannot do so effectively, then the financial portion of the case may be compromised.

Deposition Testimony

The deposition is opposing counsel's opportunity to determine what work the expert witness did, the documents and information considered, the opinions formed, and what he or she may say at trial. Preparing for a deposition is important, no matter how many times the expert witness has testified.

More specifically, the attorney taking the deposition should have the goals of:

- Evaluating the expert's qualifications
- Learning about the opinions of the expert and the basis for those opinions
- Assessing the credibility of the expert
- Locking the expert in to opinions and answers to questions
- Looking for errors in methodology or results
- Determining whether the expert exhibits bias
- Considering whether settlement is appropriate in light of the expert's opinions
- Getting an idea of how the expert will testify at trial, not just in terms of what the expert will say, but how he or she will say it and the demeanor that may be exhibited at trial

The retaining attorney and the deponent should review lines of questioning, expected responses, and difficulties that may arise during the deposition. Any potential problems with the expert's opinions or deposition testimony are best discussed in advance.

It may be helpful to provide the expert witness with the following tips, especially if the professional is relatively inexperienced when it comes to testifying:

- Pause before answering questions to carefully consider the answer and give the retaining attorney time to object.
- Answer only the question asked; do not volunteer information.
- Ask for clarification if you do not understand the question.
- Ask for compound questions to be broken down into individual questions.
- Prepare for the testimony so you are aware of key facts and remember the procedures you performed and conclusions you reached.
- Do not be afraid to ask to consult the report, notes, or other file materials before answering a question. (If the attorney conducting the deposition refuses to allow the expert to consult the file materials, it is appropriate to state the question cannot be answered without doing so.)
- Be careful when answering questions that include absolutes such as "always" or "never."

- Do not allow opposing counsel to rephrase previous answers in an inaccurate or misleading way. (Note that the expert is not required to find a second or third way to word an answer. One answer is sufficient, and any inaccurate restatement or rewording of the answer should be rejected.)
- If asked to give an opinion outside of the scope of work for which you were retained, decline to state an opinion. Also decline to give an opinion on things outside of your area of expertise.
- If asked to give an opinion on a hypothetical situation, consider it very carefully before answering. It may be that the hypothetical is unreasonable or invalid and cannot be answered.
- Do not be argumentative with the attorney asking the questions.
- Do not speculate or guess. If you do not remember something, say so; if you cannot quantify something without guessing, decline to do so.
- Be mindful of demeanor during the deposition, especially if it is being recorded by a videographer.
- Be confident without coming across as arrogant.

Following the deposition, the expert witness should review the transcript. Any inaccuracies in transcribing the expert's testimony should be officially noted so that the transcript can be corrected. If the expert notes any errors in his or her testimony, they should be brought to the attention of the retaining attorney immediately. Mistakes are sometimes made in depositions, and it is possible to note them and correct them so they do not cause problems later in the litigation.

Trial Testimony

Preparation of the financial expert should include both direct examination and cross-examination. In some cases, a judge in a family law case will ask the expert questions. These should be answered just as if one of the attorneys asked the questions on direct examination or cross-examination. When preparing for trial, some attorneys provide only minimal guidance to the financial expert, whereas others go so far as to script the questions and answers. The expert should determine what works best for him or her and insist on the appropriate level of preparation.

On direct examination, the attorney who retained the expert will question him or her to elicit the following information:

- The credentials and experience that qualify the forensic accountant to testify as an expert witness
- The work performed by the expert, including the documents and information analyzed and the procedures performed
- The conclusions drawn by the expert

To establish that the witness is an expert in the subject matter about which he or she is called to testify, the attorney should elicit some or all of the following from the testimony:

- Degrees from accredited institutions, particularly those related to the field of expertise relevant to opinions in the case
- Specialized training received
- Licenses or certifications in the field of expertise
- Membership in professional organizations
- Length of time practicing in the specialty
- Activities related to the field of expertise such as publications and speaking engagements
- Teaching courses in the specialty
- Previous expert testimony in this field of expertise

None of these things by itself prove the witness is an expert, and "performing" well will not guarantee that an expert's testimony will be admitted. However, the more of these items presented positively, the more likely the witness will be deemed an expert by the court.

In his book *The Family Law Trial Evidence Handbook: Rules and Procedures for Effective Advocacy* (American Bar Association 2013), attorney Steven Peskind points out lines of questioning by the opposing attorney that may be helpful in getting the court to reject the witness as an expert:

- Lack of education
- Improper training
- Lack of skill in performing objective testing

- Specialized knowledge not being necessary for testimony
- Inadequate information used to develop opinions
- Reliance on improper facts, procedures, or legal principles

The judge can allow the witness to testify as an expert. If the judge is not satisfied as to the expert's qualification or work as expert, he or she can either preclude the witness from testifying or limit the witness's testimony.

One of the most important parts of preparing for the forensic accountant's trial testimony is creating trial exhibits. Even though the expert's written report may be an important piece of evidence to admit at trial, the trial exhibits can be even more important. This is especially true in jurisdictions that do not allow expert reports to be admitted as evidence. Exhibits are an opportunity to concisely present the financial case with visual aids.

The visual aids may include graphs, charts, selected financial documents, or excerpts of documents or transcripts. Portions of the expert's report may translate well into trial exhibits, but new visual aids may be appropriate as well. It is important to note that some courts will allow the expert's report to be admitted into evidence, while others will not.

The key in developing effective trial exhibits is considering different learning styles. Some people learn by hearing testimony. Others learn from pictures, such as graphs. Some need to see the numbers in a chart. Others must read the evidence, such as the expert's report. The goal at trial should be to address each of these learning styles to ensure that the court will be able to fully understand the financial portion of the case.

Direct Examination

The specific questions asked of a financial expert will certainly differ for each case and will depend on the facts of the case, the assignment given to the expert, and the conclusions drawn. However, the following is a list of general lines of questioning that may be used with a forensic accountant in many family law cases.

- Background and qualifications
  - Educational background—Include both formal education and continuing professional education. Does the expert's degree relate to

the area in which he or she is expressing an opinion? (If not, how did this person obtain knowledge on this subject?)

- Credentials obtained—When were they obtained? How? (Some credentials require only a fee to be paid, while others require an application, experience in the field, and a testing process.)
- Credentials not obtained—Why not? Is the expert not qualified for them or did the expert simply choose to not get them?
- Work history related to the field of expertise
- Look for bias—Does the expert consistently work for one side or the other in cases?
- Has the expert ever been disqualified or has his or her testimony been limited?

- This engagement
  - What was the scope of the engagement? (What issues was the expert supposed to address? What work was he or she to do?)
  - Has the expert ever performed this type of work before? How many times? What was similar to or different from this engagement?
  - Has the expert ever done work in this industry?
  - Is this outside his or her area of expertise?
  - What professional standards apply to this engagement? Did the expert adhere to the standards? Can the expert articulate how and why he or she did?
  - How much time did the expert spend on this engagement?
  - Who did the work that led to the opinions? (Did the expert do the work, or was staff involved?)
  - Who prepared the report?
  - What did the expert discuss with counsel? (Try to determine how counsel may have influenced the opinions.)
  - What did the expert discuss with the parties to this case? (Try to determine what information came from the client and any influence the client may have had on the opinions.)
  - Were there any limitations placed upon the expert's work or opinions?

- Determine the materials relied on
  - What evidence and data were reviewed? Who provided the documents to the expert? (Note that there is a difference between what was looked at and what was relied on in forming opinions. That distinction may be important in any given case.)
  - Were there any documents produced that were not reviewed?
  - Is the expert aware of any documents that were withheld?
  - Did the expert ask for any documents that he or she did not receive?
- Seek details about the methodology used
  - What methodology was used? Were other methodologies considered? Why were they not used?
  - Is the methodology generally accepted by other financial experts? Who else is doing it this way?
  - Was a consistent methodology used throughout the case?
  - Were the calculations done correctly? (If any errors in calculations have been identified, point them out to the expert and ask for explanations.)
  - Is there an error rate with this methodology? What is it?
  - What is the factual basis for the expert's opinion? How do the facts lead to his or her conclusions?
  - What estimates or assumptions did the expert make? What was the basis for those estimates or assumptions? Why are they reasonable?
  - Ask about any technical terms used (to be sure that you understand their meaning and usage).
- Other work
  - Was there any other work the expert would have liked to perform for this engagement?
  - Is there any other work that the expert plans to do?
  - What outside research was conducted?
- Books and publications
  - What authoritative texts exist (related to the specific subject matter of the engagement)? What articles, periodicals, books, or treatises were relied upon?

- Are there any writings (books, articles, etc.) by the expert that may contradict his or her opinions in this case?
- Has the expert provided testimony in other cases that may contradict opinions in this case?
- Expert's opinions
  - Does the report contain all opinions that the expert plans to render at trial?
  - Are there any opinions that are not disclosed in the report?
  - Does the expert intend to form any opinions other than the ones already disclosed?
  - Do any opinions contradict previous opinions expressed in the case?
  - Are there any drafts of the expert's report? How does the final report differ from those drafts and why?
  - What does the expert agree with in the opposing expert's report? Why?
  - What does the expert disagree with in the opposing expert's report? Why?
  - What are the main weaknesses in the opposing expert's report?
  - Did the opposing expert depart from the standards of the profession? How?

Cross-Examination

During cross-examination, opposing counsel will question the expert witness, attempting to create doubt in the court's mind about the expert's opinions. He or she may try to convince the court that the expert is not qualified, and his or her opinions should not be given strong weight. Alternatively, counsel may try to attack the methods of analysis used by the expert witness or demonstrate that the opinions are faulty.

Daubert challenges (referring to U.S. Supreme Court case *Daubert v. Merrell Dow Pharmaceuticals, Inc.*, 509 U.S. 579 (1993)) are sometimes a concern. Opposing counsel tries to limit or exclude the testimony of an expert witness by challenging the methods used in coming to his or her opinions. It is important that the forensic accountant use reliable methods accepted in the community of financial experts. Opinions and conclusions should be developed with the possibility of a *Daubert* challenge in mind.

Mr. Peskind notes in his book some things to consider if opposing counsel wants to raise questions about the reliability of the expert's work:

- Bias of the expert
- Things previously written by the expert (such as articles or reports in other cases) that contradict the testimony in this case
- If certain facts assumed by the expert were untrue, how that would affect the opinions
- Methodology used by the expert
- Limitations on the expert's knowledge or experience

At all times during testimony, the expert should remain calm and answer questions clearly, concisely, and accurately. Remember that although the attorney is the client's advocate, the expert witness is not. The financial expert's role is to objectively evaluate the evidence and form reasonable, supportable opinions.

Conclusion

As is evident throughout this book, the financial issues in a divorce can be complicated, especially when there are business interests, real estate holdings, and investments owned by high-net-worth clients. The lifestyle analysis can be a very powerful weapon in the family law case when there are issues with disclosure of data and documents. Digging deep into the financial details may be necessary to uncover hidden assets and hidden income, and the lifestyle analysis is the single best way to do so.

Most cases never get to trial, and a thorough lifestyle analysis and compelling expert report will hopefully help push the case toward a fair settlement. If the case is not settled and a trial is required, a lifestyle analysis can help the court understand the financial details. If the lifestyle analysis is presented well, the goal of a fair division of assets and reasonable award of support will be more attainable.

Appendix A

Sample Form 1040, Schedule 1, and Schedule A

Form **1040**	Department of the Treasury—Internal Revenue Service (99) **U.S. Individual Income Tax Return**	**2017**	OMB No. 1545-0074	IRS Use Only—Do not write or staple in this space.

For the year Jan. 1–Dec. 31, 2017, or other tax year beginning _____ , 2017, ending _____ , 20 ___   **See separate instructions.**

Your first name and initial	Last name		Your social security number
If a joint return, spouse's first name and initial	Last name		Spouse's social security number

Home address (number and street). If you have a P.O. box, see instructions.   Apt. no.   ▲ Make sure the SSN(s) above and on line 6c are correct.

City, town or post office, state, and ZIP code. If you have a foreign address, also complete spaces below (see instructions).

Presidential Election Campaign
Check here if you, or your spouse if filing jointly, want $3 to go to this fund. Checking a box below will not change your tax or refund. ☐ You ☐ Spouse

Foreign country name	Foreign province/state/county	Foreign postal code

Filing Status

Check only one box.

1 ☐ Single
2 ☐ Married filing jointly (even if only one had income)
3 ☐ Married filing separately. Enter spouse's SSN above and full name here. ▶
4 ☐ Head of household (with qualifying person). (See instructions.) If the qualifying person is a child but not your dependent, enter this child's name here. ▶
5 ☐ Qualifying widow(er) (see instructions)

Exemptions

6a ☐ **Yourself.** If someone can claim you as a dependent, **do not** check box 6a . . . . .
b ☐ **Spouse** . . . .

If more than four dependents, see instructions and check here ▶ ☐

c Dependents: (1) First name Last name	(2) Dependent's social security number	(3) Dependent's relationship to you	(4) ✓ if child under age 17 qualifying for child tax credit (see instructions)
			☐
			☐
			☐
			☐

Boxes checked on 6a and 6b _____
No. of children on 6c who:
• lived with you _____
• did not live with you due to divorce or separation (see instructions) _____
Dependents on 6c not entered above _____
Add numbers on lines above ▶ _____

d Total number of exemptions claimed . . . .

Income

Attach Form(s) W-2 here. Also attach Forms W-2G and 1099-R if tax was withheld.

If you did not get a W-2, see instructions.

7	Wages, salaries, tips, etc. Attach Form(s) W-2	7	
8a	**Taxable** interest. Attach Schedule B if required	8a	
b	**Tax-exempt** interest. **Do not** include on line 8a . . .	8b		
9a	Ordinary dividends. Attach Schedule B if required	9a	
b	Qualified dividends	9b		
10	Taxable refunds, credits, or offsets of state and local income taxes . . .	10	
11	Alimony received	11	
12	Business income or (loss). Attach Schedule C or C-EZ	12	
13	Capital gain or (loss). Attach Schedule D if required. If not required, check here ▶ ☐	13	
14	Other gains or (losses). Attach Form 4797	14	
15a	IRA distributions .	15a		b Taxable amount . . .	15b	
16a	Pensions and annuities	16a		b Taxable amount . . .	16b	
17	Rental real estate, royalties, partnerships, S corporations, trusts, etc. Attach Schedule E	17	
18	Farm income or (loss). Attach Schedule F	18	
19	Unemployment compensation	19	
20a	Social security benefits	20a		b Taxable amount . . .	20b	
21	Other income. List type and amount _____	21	
22	Combine the amounts in the far right column for lines 7 through 21. This is your **total income** ▶	22	

Adjusted Gross Income

23	Educator expenses	23		
24	Certain business expenses of reservists, performing artists, and fee-basis government officials. Attach Form 2106 or 2106-EZ	24		
25	Health savings account deduction. Attach Form 8889 .	25		
26	Moving expenses. Attach Form 3903	26		
27	Deductible part of self-employment tax. Attach Schedule SE .	27		
28	Self-employed SEP, SIMPLE, and qualified plans . .	28		
29	Self-employed health insurance deduction	29		
30	Penalty on early withdrawal of savings	30		
31a	Alimony paid b Recipient's SSN ▶	31a		
32	IRA deduction	32		
33	Student loan interest deduction	33		
34	Tuition and fees. Attach Form 8917	34		
35	Domestic production activities deduction. Attach Form 8903	35		
36	Add lines 23 through 35		36	
37	Subtract line 36 from line 22. This is your **adjusted gross income** . . . . . ▶		37	

For Disclosure, Privacy Act, and Paperwork Reduction Act Notice, see separate instructions.   Cat. No. 11320B   Form **1040** (2017)

Form 1040 (2017) — Page **2**

Tax and Credits	38	Amount from line 37 (adjusted gross income)	38	
	39a	Check ☐ **You** were born before January 2, 1953, ☐ Blind. ☐ **Spouse** was born before January 2, 1953, ☐ Blind. **Total boxes** if: **checked ▶ 39a**		
	b	If your spouse itemizes on a separate return or you were a dual-status alien, check here ▶ 39b ☐		
Standard Deduction for— • People who check any box on line 39a or 39b **or** who can be claimed as a dependent, see instructions. • All others: Single or Married filing separately, $6,350 Married filing jointly or Qualifying widow(er), $12,700 Head of household, $9,350	40	**Itemized deductions** (from Schedule A) **or** your **standard deduction** (see left margin)	40	
	41	Subtract line 40 from line 38	41	
	42	**Exemptions.** If line 38 is $156,900 or less, multiply $4,050 by the number on line 6d. Otherwise, see instructions	42	
	43	**Taxable income.** Subtract line 42 from line 41. If line 42 is more than line 41, enter -0-	43	
	44	**Tax** (see instructions). Check if any from: a ☐ Form(s) 8814 b ☐ Form 4972 c ☐	44	
	45	**Alternative minimum tax** (see instructions). Attach Form 6251	45	
	46	Excess advance premium tax credit repayment. Attach Form 8962	46	
	47	Add lines 44, 45, and 46 ▶	47	
	48	Foreign tax credit. Attach Form 1116 if required [48]		
	49	Credit for child and dependent care expenses. Attach Form 2441 [49]		
	50	Education credits from Form 8863, line 19 [50]		
	51	Retirement savings contributions credit. Attach Form 8880 [51]		
	52	Child tax credit. Attach Schedule 8812, if required [52]		
	53	Residential energy credits. Attach Form 5695 [53]		
	54	Other credits from Form: a ☐ 3800 b ☐ 8801 c ☐ [54]		
	55	Add lines 48 through 54. These are your **total credits**	55	
	56	Subtract line 55 from line 47. If line 55 is more than line 47, enter -0- ▶	56	
Other Taxes	57	Self-employment tax. Attach Schedule SE	57	
	58	Unreported social security and Medicare tax from Form: a ☐ 4137 b ☐ 8919	58	
	59	Additional tax on IRAs, other qualified retirement plans, etc. Attach Form 5329 if required	59	
	60a	Household employment taxes from Schedule H	60a	
	b	First-time homebuyer credit repayment. Attach Form 5405 if required	60b	
	61	Health care: individual responsibility (see instructions) Full-year coverage ☐	61	
	62	Taxes from: a ☐ Form 8959 b ☐ Form 8960 c ☐ Instructions; enter code(s)	62	
	63	Add lines 56 through 62. This is your **total tax** ▶	63	
Payments If you have a qualifying child, attach Schedule EIC.	64	Federal income tax withheld from Forms W-2 and 1099 [64]		
	65	2017 estimated tax payments and amount applied from 2016 return [65]		
	66a	**Earned income credit (EIC)** [66a]		
	b	Nontaxable combat pay election [66b]		
	67	Additional child tax credit. Attach Schedule 8812 [67]		
	68	American opportunity credit from Form 8863, line 8 [68]		
	69	Net premium tax credit. Attach Form 8962 [69]		
	70	Amount paid with request for extension to file [70]		
	71	Excess social security and tier 1 RRTA tax withheld [71]		
	72	Credit for federal tax on fuels. Attach Form 4136 [72]		
	73	Credits from Form: a ☐ 2439 b ☐ Reserved c ☐ 8885 d ☐ [73]		
	74	Add lines 64, 65, 66a, and 67 through 73. These are your **total payments** ▶	74	
Refund Direct deposit? See instructions.	75	If line 74 is more than line 63, subtract line 63 from line 74. This is the amount you **overpaid**	75	
	76a	Amount of line 75 you want **refunded to you.** If Form 8888 is attached, check here ▶ ☐	76a	
	▶ b	Routing number _____ ▶ c Type: ☐ Checking ☐ Savings		
	▶ d	Account number		
	77	Amount of line 75 you want **applied to your 2018 estimated tax** ▶ [77]		
Amount You Owe	78	**Amount you owe.** Subtract line 74 from line 63. For details on how to pay, see instructions ▶	78	
	79	Estimated tax penalty (see instructions) [79]		

Third Party Designee

Do you want to allow another person to discuss this return with the IRS (see instructions)? ☐ **Yes.** Complete below. ☐ No

Designee's name ▶ _____ Phone no. ▶ _____ Personal identification number (PIN) ▶ _____

Sign Here

Joint return? See instructions. Keep a copy for your records.

Under penalties of perjury, I declare that I have examined this return and accompanying schedules and statements, and to the best of my knowledge and belief, they are true, correct, and accurately list all amounts and sources of income I received during the tax year. Declaration of preparer (other than taxpayer) is based on all information of which preparer has any knowledge.

Your signature	Date	Your occupation	Daytime phone number
Spouse's signature. If a joint return, **both** must sign.	Date	Spouse's occupation	If the IRS sent you an Identity Protection PIN, enter it here (see inst.)

Paid Preparer Use Only

Print/Type preparer's name	Preparer's signature	Date	Check ☐ if self-employed	PTIN
Firm's name ▶			Firm's EIN ▶	
Firm's address ▶			Phone no.	

Go to *www.irs.gov/Form1040* for instructions and the latest information. Form **1040** (2017)

| Form **1040** | Department of the Treasury—Internal Revenue Service (99) | **2018** | OMB No. 1545-0074 | IRS Use Only—Do not write or staple in this space. |
| U.S. Individual Income Tax Return | | | | |

Filing status: ☐ Single ☐ Married filing jointly ☐ Married filing separately ☐ Head of household ☐ Qualifying widow(er)

Your first name and initial	Last name		Your social security number

Your standard deduction: ☐ Someone can claim you as a dependent ☐ You were born before January 2, 1954 ☐ You are blind

If joint return, spouse's first name and initial	Last name		Spouse's social security number

Spouse standard deduction: ☐ Someone can claim your spouse as a dependent ☐ Spouse was born before January 2, 1954 ☐ Full-year health care coverage or exempt (see inst.)
☐ Spouse is blind ☐ Spouse itemizes on a separate return or you were dual-status alien

Home address (number and street). If you have a P.O. box, see instructions.	Apt. no.	**Presidential Election Campaign** (see inst.) ☐ You ☐ Spouse

City, town or post office, state, and ZIP code. If you have a foreign address, attach Schedule 6.

If more than four dependents, see inst. and ✓ here ▶ ☐

Dependents (see instructions):

(1) First name Last name	**(2)** Social security number	**(3)** Relationship to you	**(4)** ✓ if qualifies for (see inst.):	
			Child tax credit	Credit for other dependents
			☐	☐
			☐	☐
			☐	☐
			☐	☐

Sign Here

Joint return? See instructions. Keep a copy for your records.

Under penalties of perjury, I declare that I have examined this return and accompanying schedules and statements, and to the best of my knowledge and belief, they are true, correct, and complete. Declaration of preparer (other than taxpayer) is based on all information of which preparer has any knowledge.

Your signature	Date	Your occupation	If the IRS sent you an Identity Protection PIN, enter it here (see inst.)
Spouse's signature. If a joint return, **both** must sign.	Date	Spouse's occupation	If the IRS sent you an Identity Protection PIN, enter it here (see inst.)

Paid Preparer Use Only

Preparer's name	Preparer's signature	PTIN	Firm's EIN	Check if: ☐ 3rd Party Designee
Firm's name ▶		Phone no.		☐ Self-employed
Firm's address ▶				

For Disclosure, Privacy Act, and Paperwork Reduction Act Notice, see separate instructions. Cat. No. 11320B Form **1040** (2018)

Form 1040 (2018)   Page **2**

	1	Wages, salaries, tips, etc. Attach Form(s) W-2			1	
Attach Form(s) W-2. Also attach Form(s) W-2G and 1099-R if tax was withheld.	2a	Tax-exempt interest . . .	2a	**b** Taxable interest . . .	2b	
	3a	Qualified dividends . . .	3a	**b** Ordinary dividends . .	3b	
	4a	IRAs, pensions, and annuities .	4a	**b** Taxable amount . . .	4b	
	5a	Social security benefits . .	5a	**b** Taxable amount . . .	5b	
	6	Total income. Add lines 1 through 5. Add any amount from Schedule 1, line 22			6	
	7	Adjusted gross income. If you have no adjustments to income, enter the amount from line 6; otherwise, subtract Schedule 1, line 36, from line 6			7	
Standard Deduction for—	8	**Standard deduction or itemized deductions** (from Schedule A)			8	
• Single or married filing separately, $12,000	9	Qualified business income deduction (see instructions)			9	
• Married filing jointly or Qualifying widow(er), $24,000	10	Taxable income. Subtract lines 8 and 9 from line 7. If zero or less, enter -0-			10	
	11	**a** Tax (see inst.) _____ (check if any from: **1** ☐ Form(s) 8814 **2** ☐ Form 4972 **3** ☐ _____)				
• Head of household, $18,000		**b Add** any amount from Schedule 2 and check here . . . . ▶ ☐			11	
• If you checked any box under Standard deduction, see instructions.	12	**a** Child tax credit/credit for other dependents _____ **b Add** any amount from Schedule 3 and check here ▶ ☐			12	
	13	Subtract line 12 from line 11. If zero or less, enter -0-			13	
	14	Other taxes. Attach Schedule 4			14	
	15	Total tax. Add lines 13 and 14			15	
	16	Federal income tax withheld from Forms W-2 and 1099			16	
	17	Refundable credits: **a** EIC (see inst.) _____ **b** Sch. 8812 _____ **c** Form 8863 _____				
		Add any amount from Schedule 5 _____			17	
	18	Add lines 16 and 17. These are your total payments			18	
Refund	19	If line 18 is more than line 15, subtract line 15 from line 18. This is the amount you **overpaid** . .			19	
	20a	Amount of line 19 you want **refunded to you.** If Form 8888 is attached, check here . . . . ▶ ☐			20a	
Direct deposit? See instructions.	▶ **b**	Routing number		▶ **c** Type: ☐ Checking ☐ Savings		
	▶ **d**	Account number				
	21	Amount of line 19 you want **applied to your 2019 estimated tax** . . ▶	21			
Amount You Owe	22	**Amount you owe.** Subtract line 18 from line 15. For details on how to pay, see instructions . . ▶			22	
	23	Estimated tax penalty (see instructions) . . . . ▶	23			

Go to *www.irs.gov/Form1040* for instructions and the latest information.   Form **1040** (2018)

SCHEDULE 1 (Form 1040)	Additional Income and Adjustments to Income	OMB No. 1545-0074
Department of the Treasury Internal Revenue Service	▶ Attach to Form 1040. ▶ Go to *www.irs.gov/Form1040* for instructions and the latest information.	2018 Attachment Sequence No. 01

Name(s) shown on Form 1040	Your social security number

Additional Income

1–9b	Reserved	1–9b	
10	Taxable refunds, credits, or offsets of state and local income taxes	10	
11	Alimony received	11	
12	Business income or (loss). Attach Schedule C or C-EZ	12	
13	Capital gain or (loss). Attach Schedule D if required. If not required, check here ▶ ☐	13	
14	Other gains or (losses). Attach Form 4797	14	
15a	Reserved	15b	
16a	Reserved	16b	
17	Rental real estate, royalties, partnerships, S corporations, trusts, etc. Attach Schedule E	17	
18	Farm income or (loss). Attach Schedule F	18	
19	Unemployment compensation	19	
20a	Reserved	20b	
21	Other income. List type and amount ▶ _____	21	
22	Combine the amounts in the far right column. If you don't have any adjustments to income, enter here and include on Form 1040, line 6. Otherwise, go to line 23 . .	22	

Adjustments to Income

23	Educator expenses	23		
24	Certain business expenses of reservists, performing artists, and fee-basis government officials. Attach Form 2106 . .	24		
25	Health savings account deduction. Attach Form 8889 .	25		
26	Moving expenses for members of the Armed Forces. Attach Form 3903	26		
27	Deductible part of self-employment tax. Attach Schedule SE	27		
28	Self-employed SEP, SIMPLE, and qualified plans . .	28		
29	Self-employed health insurance deduction	29		
30	Penalty on early withdrawal of savings	30		
31a	Alimony paid **b** Recipient's SSN ▶ _____	31a		
32	IRA deduction	32		
33	Student loan interest deduction	33		
34	Reserved	34		
35	Reserved	35		
36	Add lines 23 through 35		36	

For Paperwork Reduction Act Notice, see your tax return instructions.   Cat. No. 71479F   Schedule 1 (Form 1040) 2018

SCHEDULE A
(Form 1040)

Department of the Treasury
Internal Revenue Service (99)

Itemized Deductions

▶ Go to *www.irs.gov/ScheduleA* for instructions and the latest information.
▶ Attach to Form 1040.
Caution: If you are claiming a net qualified disaster loss on Form 4684, see the instructions for line 16.

OMB No. 1545-0074

2018

Attachment
Sequence No. 07

Name(s) shown on Form 1040 | Your social security number

Medical and Dental Expenses		
	Caution: Do not include expenses reimbursed or paid by others.	
1	Medical and dental expenses (see instructions)	1
2	Enter amount from Form 1040, line 7 [2]	
3	Multiply line 2 by 7.5% (0.075)	3
4	Subtract line 3 from line 1. If line 3 is more than line 1, enter -0-	4

Taxes You Paid		
5	State and local taxes.	
a	State and local income taxes or general sales taxes. You may include either income taxes or general sales taxes on line 5a, but not both. If you elect to include general sales taxes instead of income taxes, check this box . . . . ▶ ☐	5a
b	State and local real estate taxes (see instructions)	5b
c	State and local personal property taxes	5c
d	Add lines 5a through 5c	5d
e	Enter the smaller of line 5d or $10,000 ($5,000 if married filing separately)	5e
6	Other taxes. List type and amount ▶ _____	6
7	Add lines 5e and 6	7

Interest You Paid		
Caution: Your mortgage interest deduction may be limited (see instructions).		
8	Home mortgage interest and points. If you didn't use all of your home mortgage loan(s) to buy, build, or improve your home, see instructions and check this box . . . . . . ▶ ☐	
a	Home mortgage interest and points reported to you on Form 1098	8a
b	Home mortgage interest not reported to you on Form 1098. If paid to the person from whom you bought the home, see instructions and show that person's name, identifying no., and address ▶ _____	8b
c	Points not reported to you on Form 1098. See instructions for special rules	8c
d	Reserved	8d
e	Add lines 8a through 8c	8e
9	Investment interest. Attach Form 4952 if required. See instructions	9
10	Add lines 8e and 9	10

Gifts to Charity		
If you made a gift and got a benefit for it, see instructions.		
11	Gifts by cash or check. If you made any gift of $250 or more, see instructions	11
12	Other than by cash or check. If any gift of $250 or more, see instructions. You **must** attach Form 8283 if over $500 . . .	12
13	Carryover from prior year	13
14	Add lines 11 through 13	14

Casualty and Theft Losses		
15	Casualty and theft loss(es) from a federally declared disaster (other than net qualified disaster losses). Attach Form 4684 and enter the amount from line 18 of that form. See instructions	15

Other Itemized Deductions		
16	Other—from list in instructions. List type and amount ▶ _____	16

Total Itemized Deductions		
17	Add the amounts in the far right column for lines 4 through 16. Also, enter this amount on Form 1040, line 8	17
18	If you elect to itemize deductions even though they are less than your standard deduction, check here . . . . ▶ ☐	

For Paperwork Reduction Act Notice, see the Instructions for Form 1040. Cat. No. 17145C Schedule A (Form 1040) 2018

Appendix B

Financial Discovery Checklist

A lengthy list of items that a divorce attorney should consider requesting in discovery in family law cases follows. In an ordinary divorce or child support matter, many of these items will be irrelevant or nonexistent.

This list is provided to give you a comprehensive list of items you should consider. However, this list is not exhaustive, and depending on the unique financial issues in your case, you may need to request additional items.

The basic financial documents to request or subpoena:

- All personal balance sheets and financial statements for the last five years
- Personal income tax returns (Form 1040) for the last five years, including any amended returns
- W-2s and/or pay stubs for all years for which personal income tax returns have not yet been completed or filed
- Copies of personal financial statements prepared for any purpose in the last three years
- List of all bank accounts in the party's name or to which the party has access, including the bank name, bank location, account number, and type of account
- List of all bank accounts in the party's name or to which the party had access that have been closed within the last five years, including the bank name, bank location, account number, and type of account

- List of all cryptocurrencies owned, including information on the wallet and the number of tokens or coins owned
- List of all credit cards, full account numbers, and current balances for any card in the party's name, or with which the party has charging authority (*This includes credit cards that the party uses but that are paid by a business or other entity.*)
- Detailed list of any investments, ownerships, or other interests in brokerage accounts, Treasury bills, Treasury bonds, stocks, stock options, stock warrants, bonds, debentures, guaranteed investment certificates, annuities, term deposits, bankers' acceptances, limited partnerships, commercial partnerships, joint ventures, pension plans, 401(k) plans, individual retirement accounts, employee stock option plans (ESOPs), profit-sharing plans, put options, call options, tax shelters, and any other investment of any nature, whether held directly, indirectly, or in any manner whatsoever
- List of any loans, accounts, or claims receivable with parties, terms, and full details
- Copies of all applications for credit made with banks, mortgage brokers, or any other financial institution in the preceding three years
- List of any deposits held in escrow for or by the party
- List of all safe deposit boxes in the party's name and the names of the party's nominees, including the location of each box, a list of the contents, all people with access to each box, and a schedule of all visits to the boxes in the preceding three years
- Copies of all life insurance policies
- Copies of all wills and trusts under which the party is a capital beneficiary or income beneficiary
- List of all vehicles owned or leased by the party or for the party's personal use, including automobiles, boats, snowmobiles, personal watercraft, motorcycles, and aircraft
- List of all real estate interests owned by the party directly, indirectly, or in any manner whatsoever

- Details of alterations, improvements, or renovations in excess of $5,000 made to the party's residence in the preceding three years
- Schedule of all gifts or transfers in excess of $2,500 made by the party to any individual or business entity in the preceding three years, including the recipient, the nature of the gift, the gift's value, the date of transfer, the relationship to the recipient, and any documentation related to the gift
- List of all sources of remuneration, including salaries, bonuses, stock options, expense allowances, auto allowances, club memberships, entertainment, sports events, or other compensation
- List of all persons to whom the party has given power of attorney during the preceding five years
- List of all trusts established by the party during the preceding five years, including the names of all principal and income beneficiaries

If supporting documentation for assets is deemed necessary:

- Copies of all insurance policies covering real estate, vehicles, boats, personal effects, and any other assets
- Copies of all tax assessments of real estate owned

If a detailed analysis of spending is deemed necessary:

- Copies of all bank statements, checks, deposit slips, and wire transfers for the last three (or five) years for any bank accounts to which the party has access
- Copies of all credit card statements for the last three (or five) years for any credit card in the party's name or with which the party has charging authority
- Copies of all brokerage account statements for the last three (or five) years for any brokerage accounts to which the party has access
- Electronic copy of the data file for any software used to track personal finances (such as Quicken or QuickBooks)

Documents to request if there have been any audits or other tax issues:

- Any notices of assessment or other correspondence about examinations, additional liabilities, or other disputes with taxing authorities in the last five years

Request the following documents related to business entities wholly or partially owned by either spouse:

- Business ownership records (stock certificates, charters, operating agreements, joint venture agreements, corporate minutes, or other related documents)
- Business income tax returns (Form 1065, 1120, or 1120S) for any business in which the spouse/parent has had an ownership interest for the last five years
- Financial statements for any business entity in which there is an interest, including professional practices, joint ventures, and co-ownerships, for the last five years
- Copies of valuations or appraisals done within the preceding five years
- Copies of budgets, forecasts, projections, or business plans prepared within the preceding five years
- List of all bank accounts in the company's name, including the bank name, bank location, account number, and type of account
- List of all bank accounts in the company's name that have been closed within the last five years, including the bank name, bank location, account number, and type of account
- Copies of books of minutes for companies controlled directly or indirectly by the party, including articles of incorporation, amendments, bylaws, minutes, and resolutions of shareholders and directors
- Copies of all applications for credit made with banks, mortgage brokers, or any other financial institution in the preceding three years

If a more in-depth analysis of the business entities is necessary:

- Electronic copy of the data file for any software used to track business finances (such as Quicken or QuickBooks)
- Copies of employee-related documents, including payroll records for the preceding three years, copies of fringe benefits (including insurance, medical reimbursement, or cafeteria plans), vacation policy, sick pay policy, child and dependent care plans, bonus computations, commission plans, and tuition reimbursement plans
- Copies of all employee contracts
- Copies of deferred compensation and retirement plan records, including plan documents for any pension plan, profit sharing plan, 401(k), or any other plan
- Copies of expense reimbursements forms (hard copy or electronic) and schedule of expense reimbursement payments to the employee
- Copies of buy-sell agreements
- List of all customers and copies of all major customer contracts
- Copies of lease agreements
- Copies of all notes payable
- Copies of all appraisals of fixed assets within the last five years
- Copies of depreciation schedules
- Copy of current accounts receivable aging report
- Copy of detailed inventory listing
- Schedule of investments
- Copies of all notes receivable
- Copies of documents related to all patents, trademarks, and copyrights owned by or in the process of being filed by the company

If there are questions about the legitimacy of the financial statements or tax returns of any business entity in which a spouse has an ownership interest, request:

- Copies of valuations or appraisals done within the preceding five years
- Copies of budgets, forecasts, projections, or business plans prepared within the preceding five years
- Copies of all bank statements, checks, deposit slips and deposited items, and wire transfers for the last three years
- Copies of all credit card statements for the last three years
- Copies of all brokerage account statements for the last three years
- Copies of all applications for credit with any financial institution during the preceding three years
- Access to detailed accounting records, including the general ledger, general journal, sales journal, purchases journal, cash receipts journal, cash disbursements journal, and subsidiary ledgers
- List of names, addresses, and ownership percentages of all shareholders

Appendix C

Allowable Monthly Living Expense National Standards (Effective 3/25/19)*

Expense	One Person	Two Persons	Three Persons	Four Persons
Food	$386	$685	$786	$958
Housekeeping supplies	$40	$72	$76	$76
Apparel and services	$88	$159	$169	$243
Personal care products and services	$43	$70	$76	$91
Miscellaneous	$170	$302	$339	$418
Total	$727	$1,288	$1,446	$1,786

More Than Four Persons	Additional Persons Amount
For each additional person, add to four-person total allowance:	$420

*Please note that the standards change. The Internal Revenue Service recommends that you check their website, http://www.irs.gov, periodically to ensure that you have the latest version.

Appendix D

Direct Examination Checklist

As discussed in Chapter 13, the following is a list of general lines of questioning to use with a forensic accountant during direct examination in family law cases.

- Background and qualifications
  - Educational background—Include both formal education and continuing professional education. Does the expert's degree relate to the area in which he or she is expressing an opinion? (If not, how did this person obtain knowledge on this subject?)
  - Credentials obtained—When were they obtained? How? (Some credentials require only a fee to be paid, while others require an application, experience in the field, and a testing process.)
  - Credentials not obtained—Why not? Is the expert not qualified for them or did the expert simply choose to not get them?
  - Work history related to the field of expertise
  - Look for bias—Does the expert consistently work for one side or the other in cases?
  - Has the expert ever been disqualified or has his or her testimony been limited?
- This engagement
  - What was the scope of the engagement? (What issues was the expert supposed to address? What work was he or she to do?)
  - Has the expert ever performed this type of work before? How many times? What was similar to or different from this engagement?

- Has the expert ever done work in this industry?
- Is this outside his or her area of expertise?
- What professional standards apply to this engagement? Did the expert adhere to the standards? Can the expert articulate how and why he or she did?
- How much time did the expert spend on this engagement?
- Who did the work that led to the opinions? (Did the expert do the work, or was staff involved?)
- Who prepared the report?
- What did the expert discuss with counsel? (Try to determine how counsel may have influenced the opinions.)
- What did the expert discuss with the parties to this case? (Try to determine what information came from the client and any influence the client may have had on the opinions.)
- Were there any limitations placed upon the expert's work or opinions?
- Determine the materials relied on
  - What evidence and data were reviewed? Who provided the documents to the expert? (Note that there is a difference between what was looked at and what was relied on in forming opinions. That distinction may be important in any given case.)
  - Were there any documents produced that were not reviewed?
  - Is the expert aware of any documents that were withheld?
  - Did the expert ask for any documents that he or she did not receive?
- Seek details about the methodology used
  - What methodology was used? Were other methodologies considered? Why were they not used?
  - Is the methodology generally accepted by other financial experts? Who else is doing it this way?
  - Was a consistent methodology used throughout the case?
  - Were the calculations done correctly? (If any errors in calculations have been identified, point them out to the expert and ask for explanations.)
  - Is there an error rate with this methodology? What is it?

- What is the factual basis for the expert's opinion? How do the facts lead to his or her conclusions?
- What estimates or assumptions did the expert make? What was the basis for those estimates or assumptions? Why are they reasonable?
- Ask about any technical terms used (to be sure that you understand their meaning and usage).
- Other work
  - Was there any other work the expert would have liked to perform for this engagement?
  - Is there any other work that the expert plans to do?
  - What outside research was conducted?
- Books and publications
  - What authoritative texts exist (related to the specific subject matter of the engagement)? What articles, periodicals, books, or treatises were relied upon?
  - Are there any writings (books, articles, etc.) by the expert that may contradict his or her opinions in this case?
  - Has the expert provided testimony in other cases that may contradict opinions in this case?
- Expert's opinions
  - Does the report contain all opinions that the expert plans to render at trial?
  - Are there any opinions that are not disclosed in the report?
  - Does the expert intend to form any opinions other than the ones already disclosed?
  - Do any opinions contradict previous opinions expressed in the case?
  - Are there any drafts of the expert's report? How does the final report differ from those drafts and why?
  - What does the expert agree with in the opposing expert's report? Why?
  - What does the expert disagree with in the opposing expert's report? Why?
  - What are the main weaknesses in the opposing expert's report?
  - Did the opposing expert depart from the standards of the profession? How?

Index

Uniform Commercial Code (UCC)
records, 72
Unusual expenses, standard of
living and, 30–32

Vacations, exclusion of, 31
Value of assets divided, 18
Vertical analysis, 179

W-2s, 94–96
Wages, income as, 36, 94
Wisconsin, income in, 40–44